Motorbooks International

POWERPRO SERIES

CIRCLE TRACK SUSPENSION

Forbes Aird

First published in 1994 by Motorbooks International Publishers & Wholesalers, PO Box 2, 729 Prospect Avenue, Osceola, WI 54020 USA

Motorbooks International books are also available at discounts in bulk quantity for industrial or sales-promotional use. For details write to Special Sales Manager at the Publisher's address

Library of Congress Cataloging-in-Publication Data

Aird, Forbes.
    Circle track suspension / Forbes Aird.
        p. cm.—(Motorbooks International
        powerpro series)
    Includes bibliographical references and index.
    ISBN 0-87938-872-2
    1. Automobiles, Racing—Springs and
    suspension—Design and construction. I. Title.
    II. Series.
TL257.A37 1994
629.2'43—dc20   94-941

On the front cover: Jerry Dinnen's car shows good balance as it comes out of a corner in a race on the mildly banked clay at the Flemington Speedway in Flemington, New Jersey. *Bruce Bennett*

Printed and bound in the United States of America

Contents

Acknowledgments

It might have been possible to write and illustrate this book single-handed, but that's not how it happened. Several people provided information, inspiration and help. First among these is Doug Gore, Technical Editor of *Open Wheel* magazine, who planted the seed that became chapter 10, contributed a thoughtful critique of the ideas behind chapter 8, and otherwise gave generously of his time. I am especially grateful to Doug for supplying many of the photographs reproduced here. Many other photos, as noted throughout the book, are the work of Robin Hartford, staff photographer at *Open Wheel*. Thanks to Robin, and to *Open Wheel* Editor Dick Berggren for opening the magazine's photo files to me, and for authorizing use of Doug and Robin's pictures. Thanks are also due to Dr. Lloyd Reid at the University of Toronto Institute of Aerospace Studies for confirming some of the thinking behind chapter 10, and to Brian Eggleston of de Havilland Aircraft, for a helpful discussion on the subject of airfoils in general.

I am deeply obliged, too, to the many freelance photographers who permitted their work to appear here. In alphabetical order, they are: David Allio, Bruce Bennett, Paul Cooper, Harry Dunn, Bob Fairman, John Farquhar, Gordon Gill, Jack Gladback, Barrie Goodwin, Jerry Haislip, Bill Holder, Tom MacLaren, Philip Rider, Ken Simon, and Larry Van Sickle. Sincere thanks to all these artists.

Introduction

Engines roar and scream, and get hot, and suck stuff in and spit stuff out—like a living thing.

Chassis, on the other hand, are dumb lumps; they just sit there like lawn furniture. Maybe this explains why most oval track racers find it tough to get excited about suspension and chassis technology. Or maybe it has something to do with geography. In Europe and Britain, roads existed long before cars, and to make transport practical when the only horsepower was, uh, horse power, the roads avoided grades by following river valleys and other natural features of the terrain. The cars that followed had to cope with these narrow, serpentine roads, so while there wasn't a lot of opportunity to put the hammer down, chassis science advanced rapidly.

In North America, it was the car that provided the demand for paved roads in the first place, and in the land of wide open spaces, most of those roads run straight and flat over long distances. That kind of environment places high demands on engine power and reliability, but designing a chassis to match is about as much challenge as making toast. Whatever the reasons, oval racers have inherited a tradition that for a long time has emphasized "motoring" ahead of "steering," despite the fact that track racers spend more time going around corners than they spend going straight. The resulting high degree of development in engine technology means that finding more power has become really tough, so significant reductions in lap times increasingly have to come from chassis improvements. There may be no substitute for cubic inches, but all the cubes in Rubik-land are no substitute for handling, either. This is by no means bad news, first because there is lots of room for improvement, and second because chassis work is dirt cheap compared to state-of-the-art motor mods.

Yes, Indy and Formula 1 winners use mega-dollar active suspensions and space-age composite chassis frames with space-age price tags, but there is still a lot you can do with a hacksaw, a torch... and some knowledge. In this book we are going to take a shot at filling in some of the knowledge gap, exploring the whole area of handling, suspension, and steering—the chassis, in other words. We will keep the math to a minimum, but we are going to have to be pretty theoretical at the beginning; in the same way that you can't begin to engineer or modify a motor without understanding what "compression ratio" or "valve area" means, it is wiser to leave the tube uncut and the torch unlit until you have a firm grasp on some general concepts of chassis science.

This is not a recipe book; it's a set of cooking lessons. Though we will get specific from time to time, we are never going to tell you, for instance, which right-rear spring is best for car X on track Y. We hope to provide something more valuable: the ability to figure it out for yourself! Most of this work first appeared as a series of articles in *Open Wheel* magazine between April 1989 and October 1990. That work reappears here with editorial changes, and with many new illustrations.

I welcome comments, questions, suggestions for improvement and, yes, even criticism from readers. Write to me in care of the publisher.
—*Forbes Aird*

Chapter 1

The Tyranny of the Tire

A tire forced "over the peak" of its curve of slip angle vs. normal force will give less cornering force—less "side bite." Apart from reducing cornering power, this tends to be pretty rough on the tire. *Philip Rider*

To start at the beginning, everyone understands that you can't accelerate, stop, or steer a vehicle if you are on glare ice, or flying through the air. The only way to affect the speed or direction of the car is through the grip the tires get on the ground, from being pressed into contact by the weight of the car. The primary job of race car suspension, then, is to position and load the tires so that they

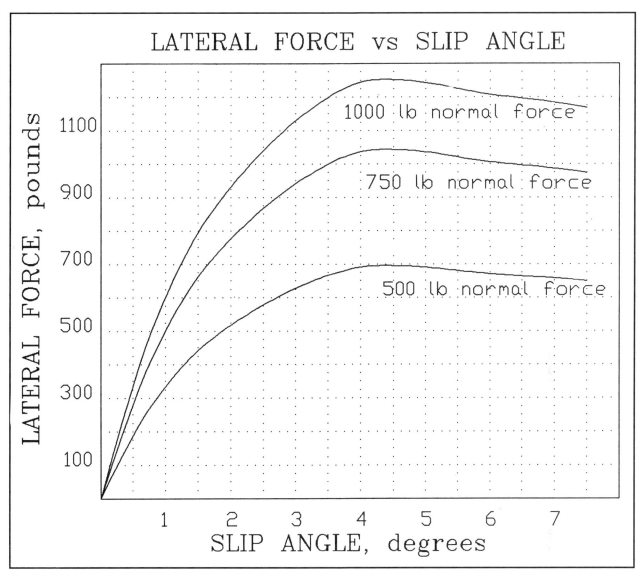

LATERAL FORCE vs SLIP ANGLE

The lateral force a tire develops depends on the slip angle. These graphs show how the side force increases at first, levels out, then falls again if the slip angle is increased beyond the peak. This data does not represent any particular tire, though the curve for a 500lb normal force is pretty close to that of one typical pavement race tire.

get the grip on the track surface that you need to control the car. This is a little different from the highest priority of passenger car suspension, which is to provide a comfortable ride, so don't be fooled into thinking that just because a race car driver doesn't object to a rough ride, the suspension system of a race car is unimportant.

Slip Angle and Lateral Force

Now, if the primary job of the race car suspension is to keep the tires in the right relationship to the road, we should look closely at the way tires work. Because a tire is flexible, it can be forced to point in one direction while it is heading in a slightly different one. The angle between the two directions is called a *slip angle*. Whenever a tire is

compelled to run at a slip angle, it will generate a force at right angles to the direction it is pointing. That is the force that shoves the car around a turn.

Various factors affect how large that force is. For starters, it depends on the size of the slip angle. Over a certain range, each small increase in slip angle results in a roughly proportional increase in the sideways shove, or *lateral force*. As the upper limit is approached, the lateral force begins to fade—increases in slip angle have less and less effect. Because the lateral force produced by a tire acts at right angles to the way the tire is pointing, rather than the way it is going, part of the lateral force acts toward the rear, tending to slow the car. It is an advantage, then, if a tire can produce the necessary lateral force at a small slip angle,

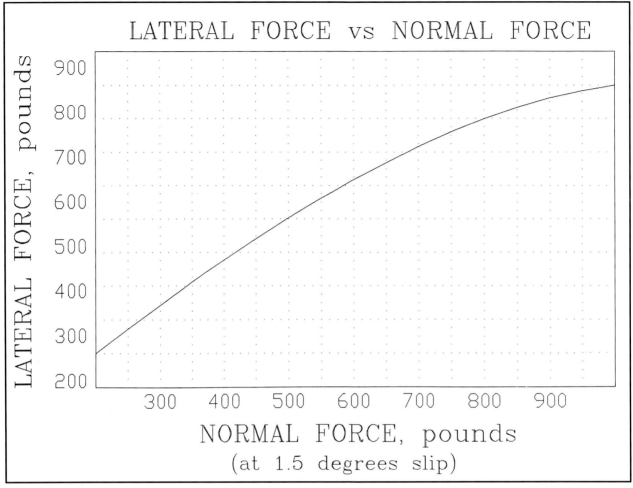

LATERAL FORCE vs NORMAL FORCE

NORMAL FORCE, pounds
(at 1.5 degrees slip)

The lateral force also depends on how hard the tire is loaded vertically. A graph of the relationship between lateral (side) force and normal (vertical) force reveals that increases in normal force yield ever smaller increases in lateral force. As a result, two tires sharing a load will develop maximum side force if they share the vertical load equally.

A moderate amount of camber when the tire is running straight can even out the pattern of load distribution across the width of the tread when the same tire is cornering hard, so that all the rubber works about equally hard.

and this characteristic is a virtue of modern low-profile race tires.

The lateral force also depends on how hard the tire is pressed onto the ground; the larger this vertical contact force—called the *normal force* by tire and chassis people—the larger the lateral force. (*Normal* does not mean standard or ordinary in this conversation. It is physics shorthand for at right angles to the road surface.) No, you don't gain anything by making the whole car heavier; you get a larger lateral force, all right, but the lump it has to push around is heavier in the same proportion. A wing, on the other hand, increases the normal force between the tire and the ground without adding anything to the weight. The effects of wings are discussed in chapters 9 and 10.

It gets awkward to keep spelling out the normal force and the lateral force in pounds for every single example you might want to look at, so tire and suspension folks talk about the *lateral force*

To even out the tire loads in left-hand turns, it is standard practice for oval track racers to start off with the weight off-set to the left side. None carry this practice further than su-permodifieds, which can start off with as much as 70 percent left-side weight. *Doug Gore, Open Wheel Magazine*

Side forces distort the tire sidewalls, increasing the load on the outside edge of the tire. A slight amount of camber when running straight can even up the loading, and the temperatures, when turning. The pattern of shading on the inside front of this Indy car shows clearly that only the inside edge is working. The more heavily worked outside front, on the other hand, is cambered just enough to compensate for tire distortion and chassis roll. *Bruce Bennett*

coefficient of a tire. The coefficient is just a number—like a percentage—that relates the side force a tire can develop to its vertical load. If a tire supporting a normal force of 1,000 pounds (lb) can develop a lateral force of 900lb, then it has a lateral force coefficient of 0.9; if it can develop 1,200lb of side force at the same vertical loading, it has a coefficient of 1.2.

It is important to realize that the lateral force produced by a tire at any given slip angle is only

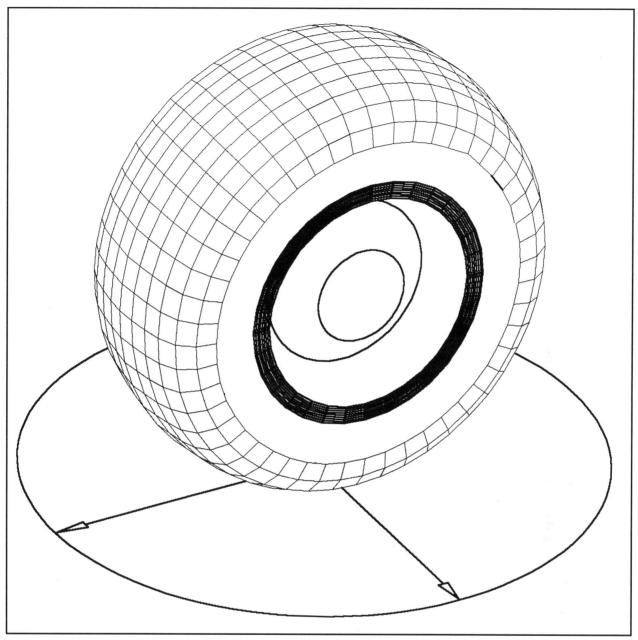

A tire can develop about the same maximum force in any direction, but it cannot produce that maximum in two directions at once. Any braking or driving thrust takes away from the cornering power available, and cornering takes away from the ability to brake or accelerate.

approximately in proportion to its vertical load. In a graph of this effect, the line showing this relationship is *nearly* straight over a certain range, but every increase in normal force yields a progressively smaller increase in lateral force, so a tire with a coefficient of 1.15 at 500lb of normal force might show a coefficient of only 1 if the load gets increased to 800lb. In other words, the coefficient gets a little smaller as the load increases.

One significant result of this is that a pair of tires sharing a load can generate the largest later-al force when they share the load *equally*. Any uneven division of the load will reduce the total force produced by the pair, since the one that is more heavily loaded will "gain" less than the other one "loses." The sharing of loads between pairs of tires can be affected in a lot of ways: offsetting weight to the left side, for example, evens up the side-to-side distribution of the load in left turns, where it counts. Later chapters discuss how to work this same vein, using tools like *anti-roll bars* (A/R bars, or sway bars), roll centers, and spring rates.

Dialing in the lateral force desired from the front tires by varying their slip angle is what every driver is doing—racer and rush-hour commuter alike—whenever he or she moves the steering wheel. And controlling the lateral force of the rear tires by use of the throttle is part of the skill of race driving.

Camber and Tire Footprint

Camber is another factor that affects the lateral force a tire can develop. When a wheel-tire assembly is tilted away from vertical, it generates a lateral force in the direction of the tilt, even when the slip angle is 0. This camber-thrust provides much of the cornering force for bicycles and motorcycles, and can really add to the cornering power of skinny street tires with a rounded tread profile. But for wide tires with flat treads and square shoulders, anything much in the way of camber angle forces the tire to run on one edge, and the reduced amount of rubber contacting the ground soon offsets any benefit from camber-thrust. Remember that tires are flexible, however, so large side forces tend to load the outside edge of a tire more than the inside. A moderate amount of camber when the tire is running straight can even out the pattern of load distribution across the width of the tread when the same tire is cornering hard, so that all the rubber works about equally hard.

The lateral force also depends on whether the tire is being asked to produce any effort in a fore or aft direction while it is cornering. A tire that is called on to produce a braking or driving thrust cannot generate as large a side force as one that is free rolling, and as this *tractive effort*—as the English call it—approaches the limit where the tire begins to spin (under power) or lock up (under braking), the potential lateral force eventually dwindles to zero. The amount of force that a tire can develop sideways is actually about the same as it can

develop forwards or backwards, so one way to describe the whole situation is to symbolize the force at the tire *footprint* (the four zones of contact between the tire and the ground) as an arrow that can be pointed to any compass heading. If the compass heading is the direction of the force, and the length of the arrow represents the amount of force available in that direction, then the arrowhead will roughly sweep out a circle. This is the *friction circle* concept you may have heard about.

Ignoring all the complicating variables, let's look at what it takes to get a car around a turn. The driver starts the whole operation by steering the front wheels relative to the rest of the car, but since the car is still charging straight ahead, this means the front tires are being forced to operate at some slip angle, so the front of the vehicle is given a sideways push in the appropriate direction. As a result, the car slowly begins to rotate—or *yaw*, as the engineers call it—around its center of gravity, so it is no longer pointing exactly the same way it is traveling. That, in turn, obliges the rear wheels to develop a slip angle of their own, which creates a corresponding sideways shove at the rear. If the shoves at the front and the back balance out to an overall push sideways, the car adopts a steady circular path.

The front wheels, though, are still steered through some angle relative to the rest of the car, so the front tires must be running at a larger slip angle than the rears, by an amount equal to the steer angle. If the back end produces the required force at a smaller slip angle than that at the front, all is well. Otherwise, the driver is obliged to back off somewhat on the steer angle to permit the stern to catch up with the bow. If the driver doesn't, the whole process winds up tighter and tighter until a complete spin-out occurs.

Dialing in the lateral force desired from the front tires by varying their slip angle is what every driver is doing—racer and rush-hour commuter alike—whenever he or she moves the steering wheel. And controlling the lateral force of the rear tires by use of the throttle is part of the skill of race driving. On the other hand, the driver has no direct control over camber or normal force, nor over most other variables that affect cornering power, like rim width, track and tire temperature, and tire inflation pressure. Once the car is on the track, nothing can be done about temperatures, rim width, or tire pressure, and, since the driver is already in charge of the steering angle and tractive effort, three variables remain under the control of the suspension system: camber, slip angles, and normal force.

Chapter 2

Camber and Slip Angles

In the last chapter we suggested that the primary job of a race car suspension system is to position and load the tires so they get an optimum grip on the track surface. Of the variables that govern the grip of a tire, three may be affected by the suspension system while the car is running: camber, slip angle, and normal force. Now we'll take a look at the first two of these and see how the suspension and steering system design can affect them, and how those effects influence the way the car handles.

In the beginning was the bump. There are two ways to drive over bumps without breaking your

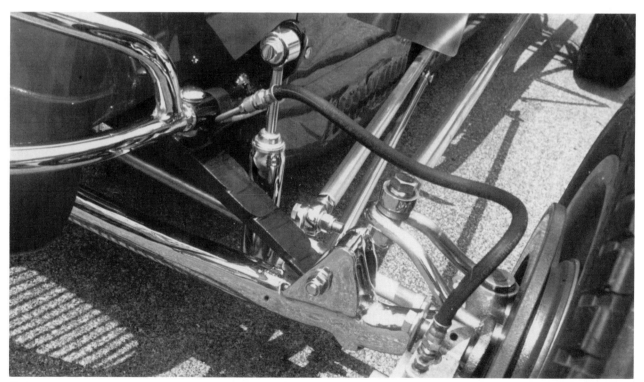

Early car suspensions were patterned after the springing arrangements on horse-drawn vehicles. One of the simplest possible arrangements is the transverse leaf spring, or buggy spring, which locates the axle from side to side but needs some additional linkage to maintain the fore-and-aft position. *John Farquhar*

teeth, or the car: you can go slow, or you can arrange for the wheels to move up and down while the rest of the vehicle more or less stays still. At an ox cart pace, you can roll solidly attached wheels over just about any kind of terrain with no problem, but if you want to go faster, you need option number two—and that's a suspension system.

When you allow the wheels to move relative to the rest of the vehicle, you need some way to control their motion so that they don't move sideways, or move fore and aft, or flop over on their side while they're moving vertically. So a suspension system consists of at least two things: a spring of one kind or another, plus some sort of hardware to control the path the wheel follows. We'll be looking at springs and their effects later, but for now, let's

The motion of one wheel of a beam axle passing over a bump is centered on the contact point of the opposite tire. Both wheels camber together. *Tom MacLaren*

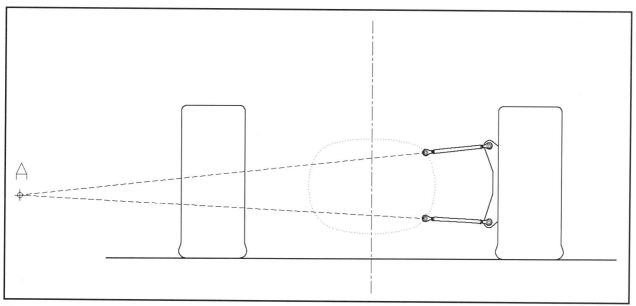

The wheel of this independent suspension will move as if connected to the chassis by an imaginary swing-axle pivoted at point *A*. The pivot point lies at the intersection of the lines of the upper and lower wishbones. As soon as the links move, a new instantaneous center is created.

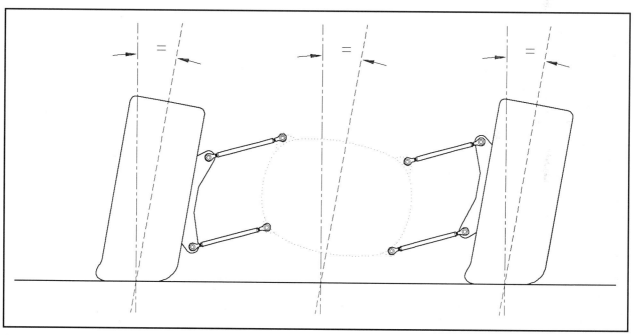

A suspension with no camber change means no camber change on roll either, so the wheels tilt sideways through the same angle as the chassis roll. The reduced rubber area alone kills a tire's cornering power; positive camber, like this, hurts even more.

consider the hardware that locates the wheels.

About the simplest form of suspension is an axle with a wheel at each end, connected to the rest of the vehicle by a leaf spring on each side running front to back. In this case, both the suspending and the locating of the wheels is performed by the leaf springs. An alternative scheme uses one leaf spring running crosswise—a "buggy spring"—which eliminates the cost and the weight of one spring but requires a bit of extra linkage to control the north-south position of the wheels. These two beam axle arrangements were in use for horse-drawn vehicles and naturally were among the earliest forms of suspension to appear on automobiles.

Steeply inclined suspension links are equivalent to a short swing-axle. This supermodified will experience a lot of camber change over a small range of vertical travel of the front wheels. *Doug Gore, Open Wheel Magazine*

For a number of strong reasons, beam axles were eventually dropped in favor of independent suspension, at least for the front end of passenger cars. Those reasons included the room a live-axle needs for vertical movement; the excessive *unsprung weight* (all the stuff that moves up and down with the wheels; the rest is *sprung weight*); and, worst of all, the existence of forces that interfere with steering.

In a race car, where a heavy rearward weight bias is sought, room is available ahead of the motor for an axle to bob up and down, so that takes care of the first complaint. Also, a contemporary oval track car using coil springs or torsion bar springs has most of its front unsprung weight in the tires, wheels, brakes, and springs; the axle itself contributes a very small fraction of the total,

On a typical wishbone independent suspension system, the change in camber with wheel movement is governed by the lengths and angles of the links, as viewed from directly in front.

which pretty much answers the second objection. The steering problem remains, which we will get to in a moment.

For all their problems, one attraction of beam axles is that the camber remains unchanged, no matter which way the chassis moves and no matter how far. Remember, camber is a tilting of the wheel—negative camber is when the top of the tire is tilted in toward the chassis, positive camber when the top is tilted the other way. Positive camber is of no benefit at all to a race car, but a little negative camber is a good thing because it usually adds a bit to the cornering power of the tire, but mostly because it helps to even out the loading on the tread rubber, as the tire tends to roll under in cornering. As long as the surface is dead smooth, this unchanging camber is a strong advantage of beam axles.

But consider what happens when the car stays still while the wheel moves. When a single wheel

Long, nearly parallel links equate to a swing-axle with a far-distant pivot center, yielding little camber change with wheel travel. *Doug Gore, Open Wheel Magazine*

Mounting the steering rack on the axle itself minimizes the worst of bump steer problems on beam axle cars. But note that the rack housing tilts with the axle, whereas the steer-ing wheel and column remain stationary relative to the car. Some bump steer error will inevitably result. *Doug Gore, Open Wheel Magazine*

Indy cars and other racers with "ground-effects" aerodynamics can tolerate very little wheel travel, so their front end suspension never operates far outside the range where it provides near-vertical wheel motion.

---

is forced up over a bump or drops into a dip, it effectively moves in an arc centered on the contact point of the tire on the opposite side, a fairly short distance away. The tilting of the axle forces both wheels to adopt, at least briefly, rather a lot of camber angle relative to the track surface. It can be argued that an independently sprung car encountering the same bump or dip would have its stability disturbed nearly as severely, but the coupling of the two wheels imposed by a beam axle so

that they both camber together also produces some bizarre steering effects.

For decades, drivers of beam axle cars learned to fear and loathe a vibration called *shimmy*. A Rolls-Royce engineer by the name of William A. Robotham discovered the root of the problem in 1925. A bump applied to one wheel of a beam front axle would cause the wheel to steer abruptly a few degrees, because of gyroscopic effects; that steering action would be communicated, through the track rod, to the wheel on the other side, which was being tilted through the same camber angle at the same time. Under certain conditions, the two wheels together would then generate a gyroscopic torque that would pick up the "down-side" wheel and slam the first wheel back onto the road surface toed-in. The whole cycle could sometimes crank up into an uncontrollable flapping of the front wheels. Though the problem can be tamed with stiff springs and shocks, and a powerful steering damper, all that stiffness defeats the purpose of a suspension system in the first place. More than anything else, it was this horror show that forced the introduction of independent front suspension. The steering fight of a beam axle remains one compelling argument for independent suspension.

On a typical wishbone independent suspension system, the change in camber with wheel movement is governed by the lengths and angles of the

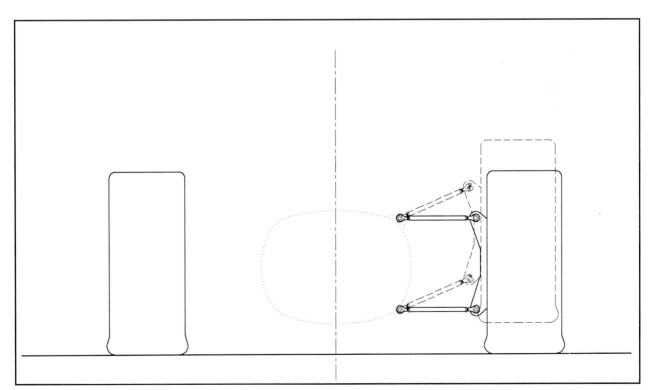

When the links are perfectly parallel, their "intersection point" lies an infinitely long way off—at a distance equivalent to the length of a swing-axle as long as the universe is wide. The arc the wheel moves in then has an infinitely large radius, so there is no tilting as the wheel travels vertically—no camber change.

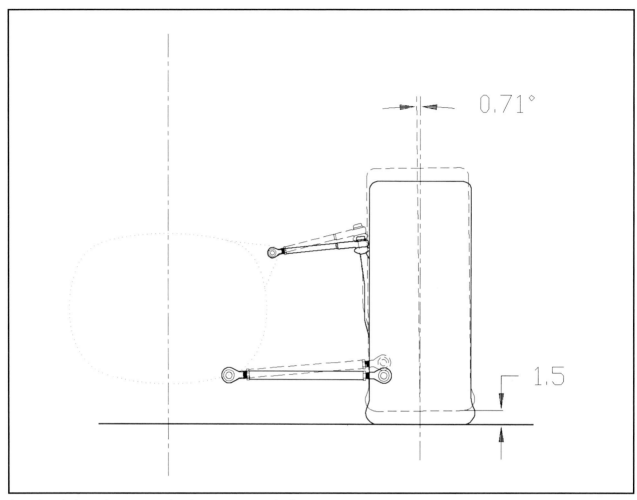

A modern independent suspension for a race car typically provides little camber gain over the first small amount of travel, partly to minimize steering fight...

links, as viewed from directly in front. Any system of two links hinged to something solid at one end and to something movable at the other end is, at any given position, equivalent to a *single* hinged link. This is true whether you're talking about the windshield wipers on a Greyhound bus or the hood hinges on your tow car or a wishbone independent suspension system. Any given position of the links has a single pivot center. You can't see it, but you can find it approximately by eyeball or exactly on a drawing board: it lies at the intersection of the lines of the links, extended until they cross.

Because this effective center of motion is determined by the angles of the links, it moves around all the time with suspension motion, so we can only talk about where it is at any given instant. For that reason, it is called an *instantaneous center*. In other words, the suspension acts just like a simple swing-axle pivoted at that center. When the links move to another position, some new instantaneous center is created, and the

wheel will move in an arc as if connected to the new equivalent swing-axle, and so on.

When the links are at a sharp angle to each other, the intersection point can be quite close to the wheel, but when the links are nearly parallel, that intersection point can lie a very long way off. In the latter case, vertical movement of the wheel is accompanied by very little camber change; the wheel is swinging around a very large arc, so almost no camber change occurs as the wheel moves. This is not the best for cornering. Certainly, the wheel remains at the same angle relative to the chassis, but because the chassis has rolled, the tire is now running at a camber angle relative to the track surface. (Of course, unless the links are also of exactly equal length, as soon as they start to move, they will no longer be parallel, so the intersection point will then move closer to the wheel.)

To achieve a useful wheel attitude when the chassis is rolled, you would have to start off with a whole lot of negative camber in the "at-rest" posi-

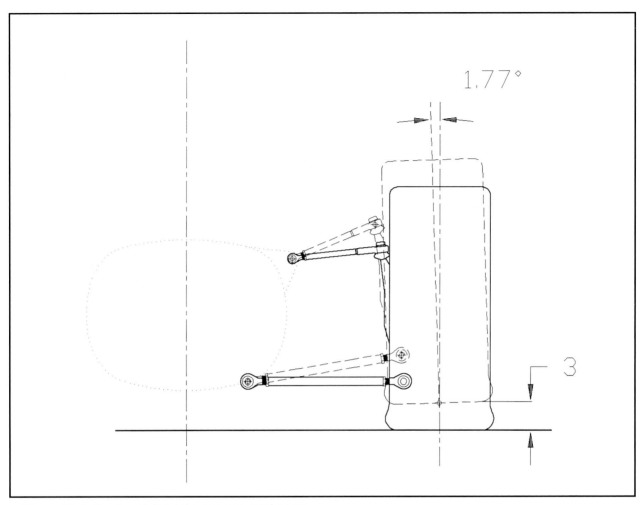

1.77°

3

... Then, with further travel, it cranks on more camber, to help keep the tire square to the track.

tion. If negative camber is carried to extremes, however, the tire will obviously be running mostly on its inside edge, which will overload and over-heat the tire on long straights—to say nothing of how it will influence traction when braking. The alternative is a linkage that changes the camber in a favorable way as the car rolls in cornering. This principle lies at the basis of suspension system de-sign for top-class race cars, including Indy and Formula One.

The usual objective is to arrange for relatively little camber change over the first small amount of wheel travel, to minimize camber change and steering kickback over typical track irregularities. Beyond this initial range, a fair bit of negative camber has to get dialed in over a relatively small amount of further motion. To achieve this, the up-per links are usually made shorter than the lower ones—much shorter in the case of the independent suspension at the rear of these cars.

Indy cars and other racers with "ground-ef-

For all their problems, one attraction of beam axles is that the camber remains unchanged, no matter which way the chassis moves and no matter how far.

fects" aerodynamics can tolerate very little wheel travel, so their front end suspension never operates far outside the range where it provides near-vertical wheel motion. What little roll occurs in the corners can easily be compensated by a modest amount of negative camber in the initial setup.

At the rear, the object is to keep the tire as square to the track as possible when accelerating, while still canceling body roll in cornering. The suspension is compressed somewhat in both cases but more so in cornering, so the linkage is arranged to increase the negative camber with upward wheel movement more so than at the front. A conflicting concern is making sure the tires do not get tipped up on one edge when the rear end rises under braking; positive camber is especially bad news. At least, rapid camber changes can be tolerated at the rear without worrying about gyroscopic kickback in the steering!

Racers running slower on rougher tracks need more than just a couple of inches of suspension travel, and may roll more, so their suspension travels farther and may experience considerable camber change at the front as well as at the rear. Since about the only place "bad" geometry can be tolerated is on rebound, it is usual to allow a fair heap of camber on a front wheel in the fully extended rebound, or *drooped*, position. Besides, if the front wheels are nearly as far down as they can get, they can't be carrying much load, so it hardly matters what the tires are doing.

Among the problems to be dealt with when the wheels have to travel a long way is the matter of bump steer. To explain: When the wheels move up and down with independent suspension, they also move in toward the car and out away from it. The steering linkage is connected to the car, though, so thought has to be given to the position of the track rods and to their length, to avoid tugging the wheels around to various steer angles as a result of suspension movement. When this undesired movement takes place as the vehicle rolls, it is called *roll steer*; when it occurs as a result of suspension travel over bumps, it is termed *bump steer*. Same thing; just different ways of looking at it.

It is easy to measure bump steer or roll steer on any vehicle: just prop the chassis up on blocks, lock the steering straight ahead, disconnect the springs, and then move the wheels through the full range of their bump-rebound travel by hand while measuring the toe-in and toe-out at regular intervals. Ideally, none should exist; what does exist must be minimized by adjusting the length of the track rods or by rearranging their static positions. If the front wheels toe out on bump or roll, that is the same as the driver winding off a little bit of steer angle when entering a turn, and will be perceived by the driver as "pushing," or *understeer*; toe-in, on the other hand, will result in a tendency for the car to exaggerate the driver's steering input, resulting in "loose," or *oversteering*, behavior.

It is possible to eliminate bump steer effects from independent front suspension by arranging for the track rods to be at exactly the same height and angle as either the upper or the lower link, and to be exactly the same length, so that movement of the suspension link is exactly shadowed by the steering link. Even when it isn't convenient to arrange this, it is usually possible—by playing with track rod length and placement—to get very close to zero bump steer over most of the range of suspension movement.

The task is much tougher with a beam axle, because no single point on the chassis—for either wheel—can be considered a fixed center of movement for both bump travel and chassis roll in cornering. In bump, each wheel arcs around the contact point of its mate on the other side; in roll, the center of motion is at or near the middle of the car. Another problem: with typical "four-bar" linkage, the axle steers bodily whenever either wheel moves up or down. Because the center of this movement almost never coincides with a joint in the steering linkage, a further steering error gets added to the axle steer.

What happens at the front can at least be grappled with by the driver, but the rear wheels can steer too! This is a tough one to beat with a beam rear axle, and you're also stuck forever with a fixed amount of rear camber and toe-in or -out (usually zero, though it is possible to "gronk" a live rear axle housing to provide some fixed amount of either). Also, unlike the front end, a live rear axle does have a problem with unsprung weight. There is a lot to be said, then, for independent rear suspension.

Left
On an independent front suspension, bump steer can be minimized by tinkering with the position, length, and angle of the track rod. Dial gauges contacting a plate bolted to the hub allow measuring the amount of bump steer as the wheel is moved through the range of vertical travel. Removing the springs makes this task easier! *Paul Cooper*

Chapter 3

The Basic Nature of Springs

In the previous chapter we talked about the ways that beam axles and independent suspension systems affect the positioning of the tires on the road surface, in terms of camber and steer angle. These are two of the three factors that are under the control of the suspension while the car is on the track. The third variable under the control of the suspension while the car is on the track is the vertical contact force between the tire and the ground. This last one is a lot trickier than it looks, so rather than jump right in, we're going to pause here to review the basic nature of springs.

In the priorities of most racers, ride quality probably rates right up there in significance with the color of the upholstery. In fact, since black seats get bleeping hot in the sun, upholstery color probably gets the nod, as far as importance. But there are two points to be made about ride quality. The first is that anything that beats up the people also beats up the car; bash hard enough, and you'll break something. The second point is that ride comfort and tire grip and stability are all connected in some ways.

When a spring is loaded, it deflects a certain distance, according to the size of the load. This relationship between force and distance is the *spring rate*, and is expressed in terms of pounds per inch of travel. Big numbers mean stiff springs; small ones make for soft springs. A 400-pounds-per-inch spring, for example, will deflect 1/2 inch (in) under a 200lb load, 1in under a 400lb load, 2in under an 800lb load, and so on.

Most springs have this kind of constant rate, but coil springs can be made from tapered wire (very rare) or formed into a sort of barrel shape or wound with a finer pitch at one end than at the other, so that some coils become bound up solid after a small amount of movement, shortening the effective length of the spring and forcing the rate higher. This same *progressive rate* effect is present to some extent in arrangements, including most "coil-overs," where regular coils have their end turns closed to provide a flat seating.

The compromise between soft springs and hard ones is very much a compromise between minimizing stresses in the structure and minimizing disturbance to the handling on the one hand, and controlling roll and pitch and movement of the unsprung parts on the other hand.

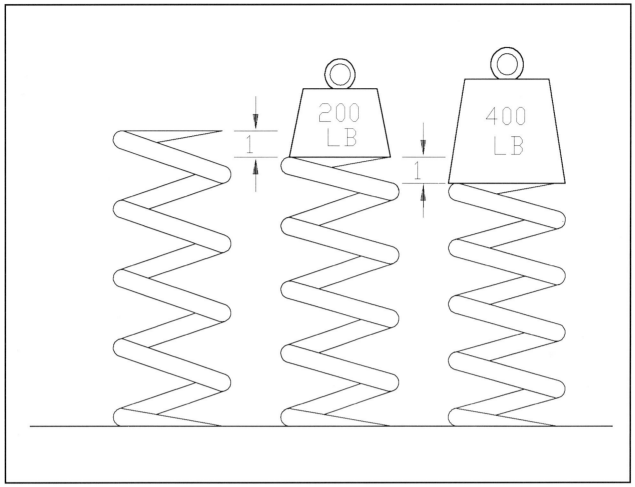

For a conventional spring, each equal increase in force compresses the spring by the same amount. The load in pounds for 1 in of spring travel is the *rate* of the spring.

It is important to realize that the only spring rate that counts is the rate measured at the wheel. For instance, if a coil is installed at an angle to vertical, it will not compress as far as the actual wheel movement. Also, only part of the force of the spring is acting straight downwards; the rest of it is trying to stretch the axle or suspension link. Both effects make the coil behave like a softer spring, acting straight up and down at the wheel.

Similarly, changing the length or angularity of the lever arm that connects a torsion bar to the suspension doesn't do anything to alter the nature of the torsion bar itself, but it does alter the leverage the suspension gets on the spring, so it effectively changes the wheel rate.

With all that in mind, consider what happens to a wheel carrying 400lb of weight when it is driven upwards—say, 1in—by a bump. If the spring rate, measured at the wheel, is 200lb per inch, then in addition to the 400lb force that is holding the car up, the spring will now be pushing up on the chassis with an *additional* force of 200lb. If that happens at each wheel at the same time, everything in the car will be accelerated upwards at 0.5 force of gravity (G), and the loads on every mounting in the car will momentarily increase by 50 percent. A 2in bump will double the force increase; a 1/2in bump will halve it. Similarly, "stiffer" springs—that is, springs with a higher spring rate—will increase the loads in the structure in proportion to the increase in stiffness, whereas "softer" springs will lower the loads. Soft springs permit lighter construction, or, for the same weight, give a larger margin of structural safety. This is the first argument for soft springs.

Meanwhile, at the other end of the spring, the tire that was being held onto the track by its 400lb share of the total weight of the car has that load increased—briefly but suddenly—by 200lb, for a total of 600lb. This is extremely significant if the car is cornering when the bump occurs, because, as shown earlier, the side force a tire can develop de-

In the priorities of most racers, ride quality probably rates right up there in significance with the color of the upholstery. In fact, since black seats get bleeping hot in the sun, upholstery color probably gets the nod, as far as importance.

pends on how hard the tire is pressed onto the ground. The larger the vertical contact force (the normal force) the larger the lateral force.

If the tire we've been talking about has a lateral force coefficient of 1.5—that is, if it can develop a maximum side force one-and-a-half times larger than the ground contact force—then just before the bump, it would have been pushing the car sideways, around the turn, with a force of 600lb. But for the brief moment it passes over the bump, that force gets increased.

It takes a little time—the best part of a full revolution of the wheel—for the tire to work its way up to a new, greater side force in response to an increase in vertical loading, so the change in lateral force will not be instantaneous. Because ordinary bumps don't last that long, the tire will never stabilize at the new value of normal force. Still, it will get partway in its adjustment to the new situation, so a momentary variation in vertical force will definitely cause a hiccup in the lateral force. This obviously does not help stability in the corners, and is the second reason soft springs are valuable in racing.

Though most race cars run with springs that would be considered very stiff by passenger car standards, it can be argued that they are as soft as they can be without running into even worse problems than the violent, rapidly changing forces we've described.

What could be worse? Well, even more violent forces, for one thing. If all the suspension travel gets used up by pitch (forward, under braking, or backward, under acceleration), by roll, or by being

Left
Many passenger cars use tapered, barrel-shaped springs to give a progressive rate—it increases with travel. *Robin Hartford, Open Wheel Magazine*

Coils with closed ends, like the one on the right, also stiffen up slightly after the end turns close-up solid. *Doug Gore, Open Wheel Magazine*

squashed under the vertical loading of a wing, then the only springing available is whatever is allowed by the flexing of the tire and frame. The spring rate will rise to astronomical levels, and the structural and handling problems will become intolerable. So one reason stiff springs are adopted is to prevent the even greater stiffness of bottomed suspension.

Another factor that limits how soft springs can be is the need to control wheel movement. After a wheel has been shoved up over a bump (or when it encounters a dip), it doesn't just fall down under its own weight—it is pushed back down by the spring, at a speed that depends on how fast the spring can accelerate it. Acceleration is just a matter of force and mass, so for a given weight of wheel and tire, and all the other unsprung weight, a stiff spring

The spring rate measured at the wheel depends not just on the spring, but also on the leverage it gets on the wheel. Slanted springs like these give a lower installed rate than springs arranged vertically. *Doug Gore, Open Wheel Magazine*

will accelerate the wheel faster than a soft one, and it will regain contact with the track quicker.

The compromise between soft springs and hard ones is very much a compromise between minimizing stresses in the structure and minimizing disturbance to the handling on the one hand, and controlling roll and pitch and movement of the unsprung parts on the other hand. Whatever the spring rate, a reduction in unsprung weight always helps with keeping the wheels on the ground. If the unsprung parts are made lighter, the spring will have an easier time getting the tire planted back on the ground after a disturbance, so a softer spring can be used. At the same time, pitch can be reduced by anti-dive and anti-squat geometry, and roll can be kept under control by careful planning of roll center heights—aspects of the suspension design that we'll get to later. Another way to minimize the chassis roll that soft springs permit is to use A/R bars. These are just torsion bar springs that connect wheels on opposite sides of the car and thus fight movement of one wheel relative to the other but have no influence when both wheels are deflected together, as when passing over a step

or ridge that affects both wheels at the same time.

What is a spring, anyway? Nothing is infinitely stiff; every part of a structure deflects somewhat whenever a force is applied to it, so in some sense, everything is a spring. The distinguishing feature of *intentional* springs is that the material is arranged so that the force has to act on a considerable length of it. That way, the deflection of each bit gets added to that of the next, and a large amount of movement takes place in response to a relatively small applied force. Thus, springs essentially trade force for distance.

Even though their shape is arranged to allow maximum movement for a given amount of stress in the material, the stresses in springs are very high, and demand first-class material. In fact, *spring steel* is a term often used to signify top-quality material, wherever it may be used. A popular

Right
Compare this with the previous photo. In this installation, the wheel rate will be very close to the actual spring rate. *Doug Gore, Open Wheel Magazine*

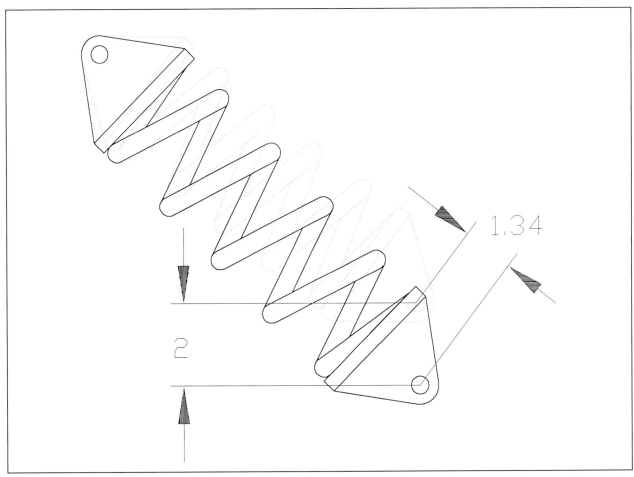

A spring installed at an angle does not travel as far as the wheel does, and part of its force is spent acting sideways instead of vertically. This reduces the rate of the spring measured at the wheel.

Though most race cars run with springs that would be considered very stiff by passenger car standards, it can be argued that they are as soft as they can be without running into even worse problems than the violent, rapidly changing forces we've described.

material for springs is chrome vanadium steel, though some people still swear by manganese silicon steel. Chrome moly steel, like 4340 or 4130, is often used to make A/R bars, and 4340 is used in some coil springs and torsion bar springs. The very best springs are made from chrome silicon steel. Coil springs should preferably have their end coils closed and ground flat to give them secure seating, and all coils and torsion bars benefit from shot-peening, which reduces the chance of surface cracking. Mercedes-Benz Formula One cars used to wrap electrical tape around their highly polished, highly stressed torsion bars, to provide a degree of additional protection against minor scratches from flying rocks, dropped wrenches, and so forth.

From the point of view of the wheels, it doesn't matter much whether the springs are coils, leaves, or torsion bars. From the builder's perspective, the choice between coils and torsion bars is very much a matter of personal preference and of how conveniently the installation fits the rest of the design of the car. Coils are simply torsion bars wound into a spiral. Leaf springs, on the other hand, do not use

A torsion bar has to be operated by a lever. Though the rate of the bar doesn't change, altering the length of the lever arm will affect the wheel rate. *Doug Gore, Open Wheel Magazine*

Though most coil-overs are "direct acting," they too are sometimes operated by a lever. Again, the geometry of the installation determines the spring rate as much as does the basic nature of the spring. *Doug Gore, Open Wheel Magazine*

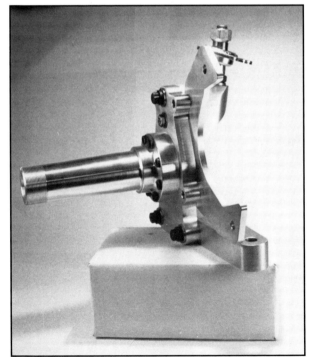

Above and opposite page
The use of lightweight suspension and brake components to reduce unsprung weight allows softer springs to be used without any loss in control of wheel motion over bumps. *Willwood Disc Brakes (brake photos); Coleman Machine (hub); and Robin Hartford, Open Wheel Magazine (wheel)*

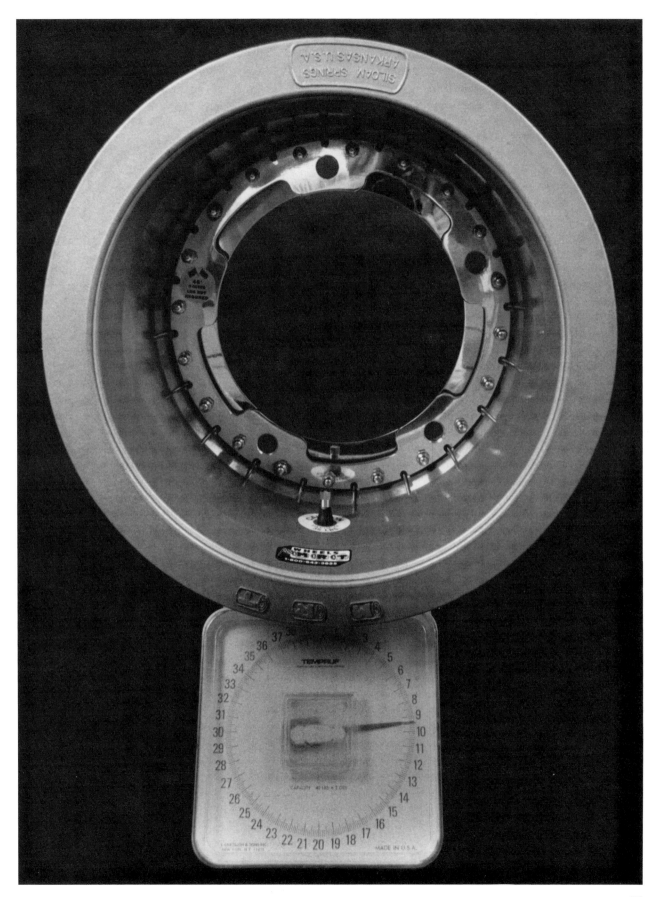

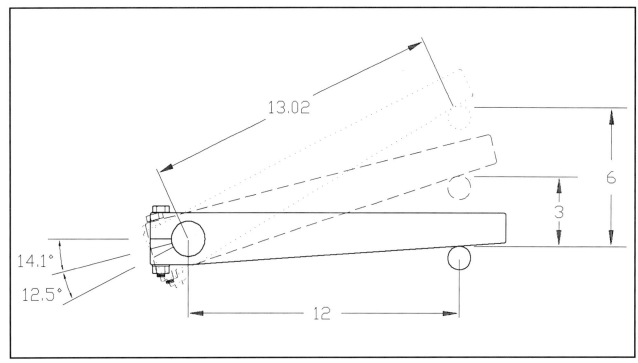

Depending on the arrangements of the linkage used, the second inch of wheel travel may not twist a torsion bar as far as the first inch. The working length of the lever may also increase, which exaggerates this effect, so the spring rate measured at the wheel is progressively reduced...

their material as efficiently as coils or torsion bars, so they necessarily weigh more. In the case of springs, efficiency is measured in terms of how much energy the spring can store for each unit of weight. Some comparisons can be seen in the accompanying table in this chapter.

Spring Material and Configuration
Energy Storage (ft-lb/lb)

Steel coil or torsion bar	66
Steel leaf	17
Composite leaf	70
Rubber, compression or shear	150–250
Rubber, tension	500+

ft-lb/lb = foot-pounds per pound

In truth, a few more considerations are involved in the choice between coils and torsion bars. For one thing, whereas a similar alternative is impractical for coil springs, you can reduce the weight of a torsion bar for a given amount of energy storage by using a hollow bar of slightly greater diameter.

On the other hand, because a torsion bar has to be twisted by a lever arm of some sort, any suspension movement will change the leverage the arm gets on the bar. Usually, the leverage increases the farther the wheel moves, reducing the effective spring rate. This gives stiffer springing over small disturbances and softer springing over large ones—just the opposite of what is wanted. It is possible to arrange things to give the opposite effect, but if the torsion bar lever forms part of the suspension, this kind of progressive action may require a position for the torsion bar that gives unfavorable axle steer.

Finally, as can be seen from the accompanying table, though ordinary steel leaf springs have to weigh about four times as much as coils or torsion bars doing the same job, a leaf spring made of composite material, like those on a Corvette, actually more than makes up the penalty. Also, in leaf spring installations where the spring serves double duty by providing a locating function as well as the springing, some of the weight of the leaf can be counted against the suspension links it replaces. In these cases, you can figure that the effective link length is about three-quarters of the length of the leaf, from the eye to the clamped part.

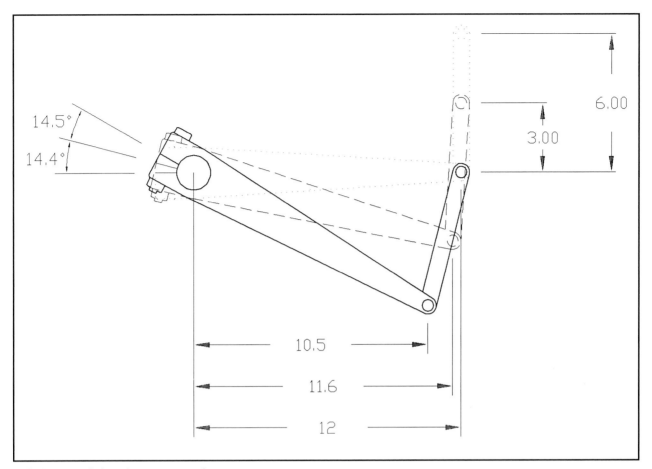

... Or it can work the other way around.

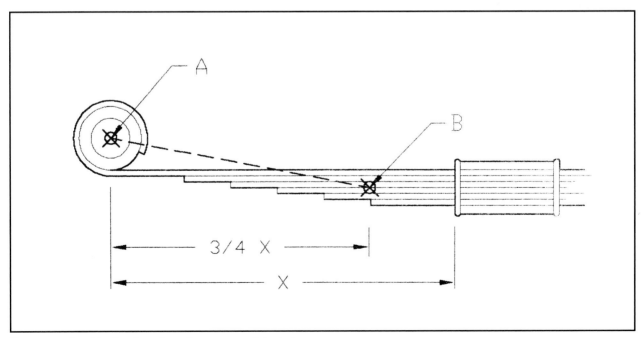

For conventional leaf springs that also serve as links to locate the wheels, the equivalent link is approximately as shown here by the line *A–B*.

Though leaf springs are less efficient than coils or torsion bars, the use of modern composite materials can more than make up the difference. Note the fiberglass spring on this supermod. *Doug Gore, Open Wheel Magazine*

Chapter 4

Tire Loads in Corners

Now that we've considered how springs can affect tire contact forces while the car is going in a straight line, we can deal with the effects the suspension has on tire loading in corners. Cornering forces originate at the tire footprints—the four zones of contact between the tire and the ground—so the force that pushes a car around a turn acts at ground level. The mass of the car is all above the ground, though, so the side forces are being applied below the center of gravity. This offset between the line of the force and the mass it is acting on results in a torque called the *overturning moment*, that tends to make the car tip over toward the high side. The effect of this overturning tendency is to transfer weight from the inside wheels to the outside wheels.

This load transfer to the outside tires in a turn does not depend on the suspension system. For example, if you drive in a circle at ever-increasing speeds in a vehicle with no suspension at all—like a go-cart—the inside wheels will get lighter and lighter and they will eventually begin to lift off the track, assuming the tires and track are sticky enough. At this point, all the weight of the vehicle is obviously on the outside tires, so you have 100 percent weight transfer, and suspension has nothing to do with it. The total load transfer from the inside to the outside pair of tires depends only on the radius and speed of the turn, the track width of the vehicle, and the height of the vehicle's center of gravity.

The suspension affects the share of that load transfer taken by the front versus the rear. Think about that go-cart again, but modify it this time. Imagine a new front end arrangement consisting

Soft springs are desirable to minimize stresses on the chassis and disturbances to the stability of the car, but they may lead to excessive roll. Why not just raise the roll centers to reduce or even eliminate roll?

of an axle secured to the front cross-member by a single bolt in the middle, like the nose of an old Farmall tractor, so that you could pick up the front of the vehicle and spin the axle around like a propeller. Leave the rear end solid.

Now, repeat the experiment of driving around in a circle. Eventually, the inside rear wheel will lift, telling you that tire is carrying no load at all. But because the vehicle can roll around the mounting bolt for the front axle without lifting a front wheel, the inside front will stay planted on the ground, which means that it is carrying some load. In fact, if you could get the swivel bolt right down to ground level, you would discover that the inside front is carrying the same load it was when the vehicle was standing still. All the weight transfer is

Wings—or, more particularly, their endplates—confound the analysis of race car handling. Apart from aerodynamic effects, the forces that shove a car around a turn originate at the areas of contact between the tires and the ground— look at the distortion of the rear tires, especially on the lead car. *Harry Dunn*

Cornering forces originate at the tire footprints—the four zones of contact between the tire and the ground—so the force that pushes a car around a turn acts at ground level.

taking place across the rear pair of tires.

Recall from chapter 1 that the cornering force a tire can deliver depends on how hard the tire is pressed onto the ground. More vertical load yields more cornering force, but the connection isn't perfectly proportional: every increase in vertical force yields a progressively smaller increase in side force. As a result, a pair of tires sharing a load can develop the greatest cornering power when they share the load equally. Any uneven distribution of load between them will reduce the total cornering power of the pair, because the one that is more heavily loaded will gain less than the other one loses.

In the case of our imaginary test vehicle, all the load transfer is being taken by the rear tires, so their total cornering power is reduced relative to that of the front pair. If the side force available from the rear fades while that from the front remains the same, the vehicle's handling is going to be really loose. Putting the rear axle on a swivel

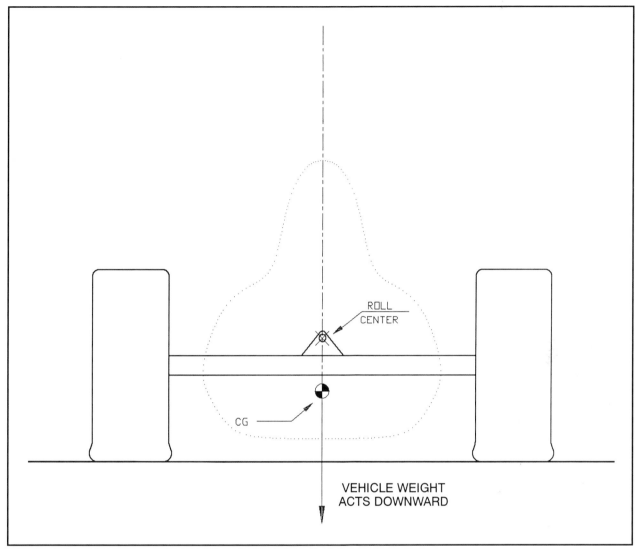

ROLL
CENTER

CG

VEHICLE WEIGHT
ACTS DOWNWARD

If the roll center is above the center of gravity, the car will simply "hang" from the pivot point.

and leaving the front end solid would have exactly the opposite effect.

If we fitted a swivel-mounted axle at *both* ends, with the pivots near ground level, the vehicle would obviously fall over on its side. But if we got the swivel centers up high enough—above the center of gravity—the vehicle would just hang there, suspended. In fact, this is the origin of the word *suspension*; arrangements like this were used in horse-drawn coaches. When such a vehicle goes around a turn, the side force is applied to the body *above* the center of gravity, so the body leans *into* the turn, like a motorcycle. We could also fiddle around until we got the swivel points at exactly the same height as the center of gravity. Then, cornering would have no effect on the attitude of the body, and if it weren't for the problem of knotting the steering linkage and the brake hoses, we could

walk up to the car and spin it around just like a chicken on a rotisserie skewer. In both cases, however, the load transfer would still be toward the outside of the turn, and eventually, the inside wheels would lift, just as with the solid suspension go-cart.

We can also imagine that we might arrange for the front and rear pivots on our theoretical test vehicle to be at different heights. Remembering that these joints are the only connection between the tire forces and the mass of the car, realize that the higher the swivel joint, the more "leverage" the mass gets on the axle—the end with the higher pivot will be the first to lift a wheel. That end, then, will take the larger share of the load transfer, so it will tend to wash out first in cornering, all other things being equal.

Let's consider a simpler situation where both

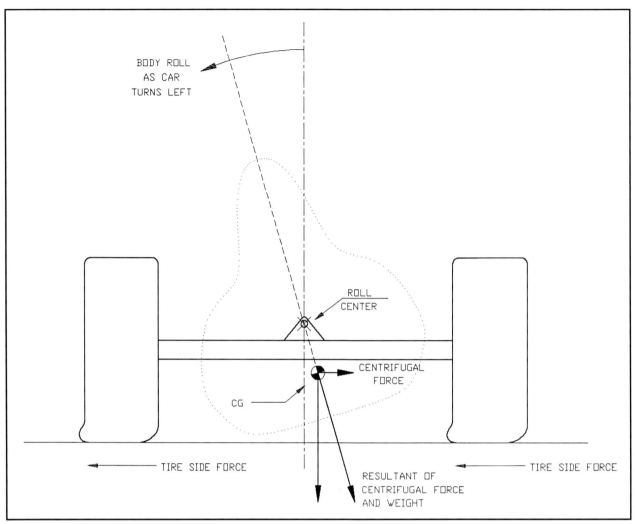

BODY ROLL
AS CAR
TURNS LEFT

ROLL
CENTER

CENTRIFUGAL
FORCE

CG

TIRE SIDE FORCE

TIRE SIDE FORCE

RESULTANT OF
CENTRIFUGAL FORCE
AND WEIGHT

If the roll center is above the center of gravity, side forces will make the body swing inwards in turns. Nevertheless, weight transfer still loads up the outside tires and reduces the load on the inside tires.

front and rear pivots are at the same height. We've seen that if the center of gravity is above the line connecting the pivots, the vehicle will tend to fall over on its side. One way to resist that tendency is to fit springs. Note that this doesn't provide a suspension system in any usual sense—the axles are not free to bounce up and down, they can only swivel around the mounting bolts, and the springs don't do anything to improve the ride, they just keep the vehicle from falling over.

When centrifugal force makes the body try to roll around the pivots, the springs on the outside are compressed and they fight back, until an equilibrium is reached. The car will roll in corners, just like a real car with real suspension. As long as the pivots are above the ground but below the center of gravity, part of the overturning moment will still be carried through the pivots, but the rest will now be resisted by the springs.

Most real cars roll toward the outside of a

turn—though aerodynamic forces can make winged sprint cars roll inwards, as discussed in chapter 10. If you were to take a photograph of a car leaned over from cornering, seen head-on, and compare it with a similar photograph of the car standing still, you could measure the angle of roll, and you could also estimate the location of the point the car is rolling around. That point is the *roll center*. In the case of our "swivel-axle" experiments, the roll center is the mounting bolt. In real-world suspension systems, the roll center may be an actual swivel point—the center pivot of a Watt's linkage, for instance—but usually it is just an imaginary point in space, its location determined by the geometry of the suspension linkage.

The center of roll may be on the centerline of the car at ground level, or it may be above or below the ground by a significant distance. It might also be offset sideways from the car centerline, but that is a complication we won't go into. On the front

When centrifugal
force makes the body try to
roll around the pivots, the springs
on the outside are compressed
and they fight back, until an
equilibrium is reached.
The car will roll in corners.

suspension of most passenger cars, for example, the roll center is below ground level, sometimes by several inches. On most race cars, the front roll center will be anywhere from a couple of inches to 8in or 10in above the ground. At the rear, most live-axle arrangements produce a roll center near axle height. Independent rear setups usually have somewhat lower roll centers. Note that a car doesn't have just a single roll center—it has two, one for each end, just as if it had two swivel bolts. The car actually rolls around an imaginary line connecting the two roll centers, called the *roll axis*.

Back to the track with our imaginary test car... with a real suspension system this time. Let's say each wheel carries the same load, and the roll center heights are the same at each end, but below the mass center (this is almost always the

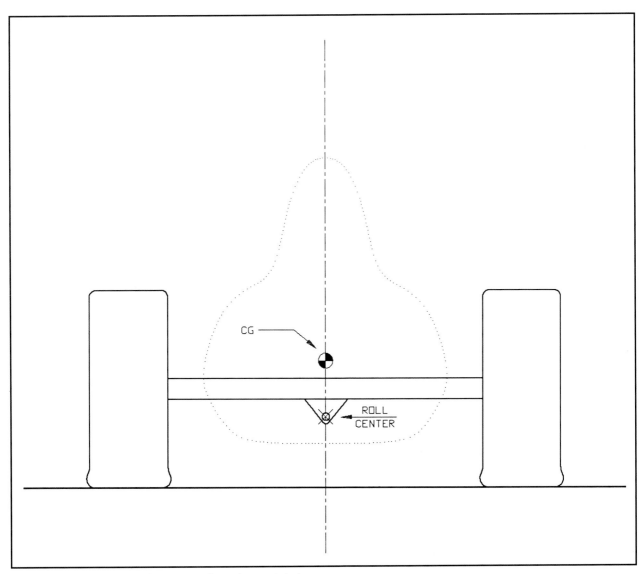

If the roll center is below the center of gravity, as it is in most race and street cars...

case for both race and street cars), so the springs have to resist the tendency of the body to roll when cornering. Since the chassis of the car does not twist much, the roll angle must be virtually the same at both ends of the car, so both sets of springs will be compressed the same amount.

If we have put stiffer springs on one end, that end will resist the rolling more than the "softer" end will, so even though the amount of load transfer carried through the roll centers is the same at both ends—remember, they are both at the same height—the end with the stiffer springs will carry more than half of the remainder. The tires at that end will experience a greater imbalance in loading, and that end will lose grip first. Similarly, if we fitted identical springs at both ends but changed the height of one of the roll centers, the end with the higher roll center would take more of the load

transfer and would wash out first.

If you remember that the *total* load transferred through the springs and through the roll centers must always add up to the same number, you can see that as the one increases, the other decreases. The portion that acts through the roll centers will be distributed front to rear according to the roll center heights at each end and the fore-aft weight distribution. The portion that acts through the springs is split in proportion to the stiffness of the springs.

Any difference in the way load transfer is handled at opposite ends of the car will affect whether the car understeers (pushes) or oversteers (gets loose), so messing around with roll center heights and spring rates sounds like a basic and convenient way to modify the handling of a race car. It is, but there is more to it than that. For instance,

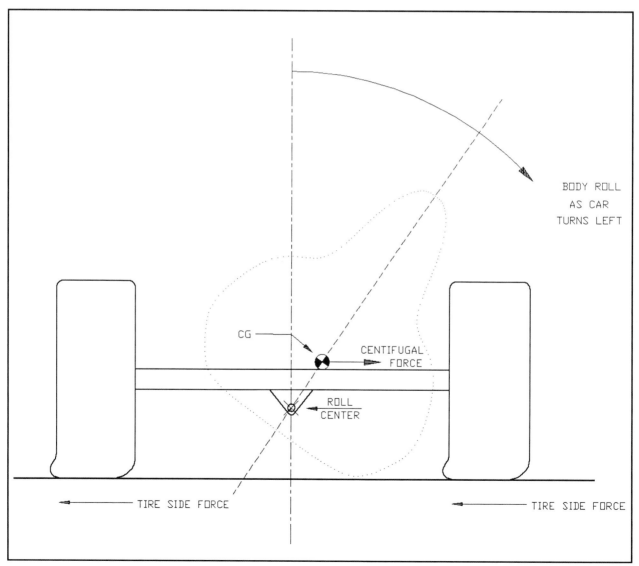

... the car will just fall over on its side...

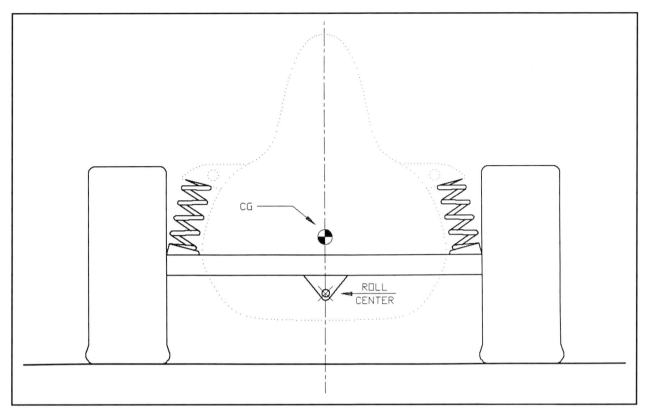

CG

ROLL
CENTER

... unless we fit springs. Side forces will transfer load partly through the roll center...

⚑⚑

Any difference in the way load transfer is handled at opposite ends of the car will affect whether the car understeers (pushes) or oversteers (gets loose).

---

soft springs are desirable to minimize stresses on the chassis and disturbances to the stability of the car, but they may lead to excessive roll. Why not just raise the roll centers to reduce or even eliminate roll?

Though the details differ between beam axle suspensions and independent setups, high roll centers have some serious drawbacks in both cases. Roll centers work two ways: they are the points that define the motion of the body relative to the wheels, but they also help define the motion of the wheels relative to the body. On a beam axle setup, when a wheel encounters a bump, the axle tilts. If the roll center is located some distance above the ground—and it's hard to imagine how it could be otherwise—it will be forced to move sideways as the axle moves in an arc around the far tire.

This lateral shove to the car may cause the tire to break traction, especially if it is being worked very near the limit of its grip. It also will cause a rougher ride and greater stresses in the suspension and chassis structure. On independent setups, no mechanical point defines the roll center—it is determined by the geometry of the suspension links. But any conventional linkage arrangement that gives a high roll center also causes a similar lateral movement, though the effect only occurs at one wheel.

Leaving the roll centers near ground level, on the other hand, will require very stiff springs to control roll. And using differences between front and rear springs to tune the handling may lead, for instance, to springs at the front being stiffer than those at the rear. This may cause serious problems with pitching, or "porpoising," over bumps.

It should be obvious by now that the selection of roll center heights and spring rates is a compro-

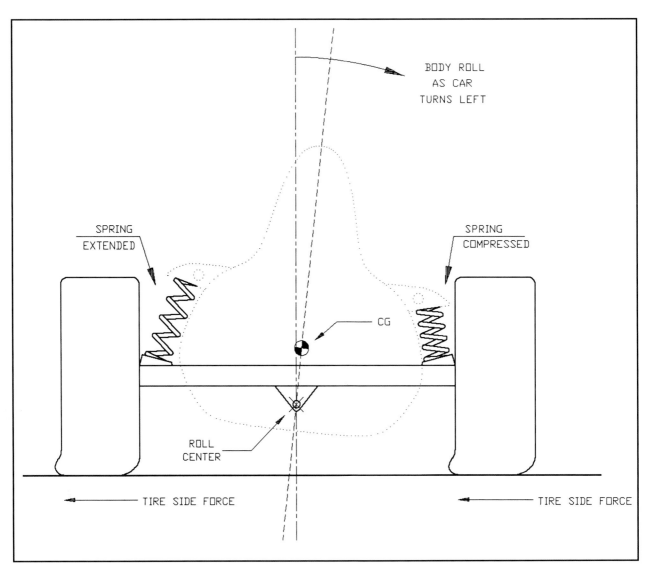

BODY ROLL
AS CAR
TURNS LEFT

SPRING
EXTENDED

SPRING
COMPRESSED

CG

ROLL
CENTER

TIRE SIDE FORCE

TIRE SIDE FORCE

... and partly through the springs. The springs on the outside will be compressed as a result. The total roll angle will depend on the share of overturning force carried by the springs, and on their stiffness.

Right
Remove the aerodynamic effects, and the underlying truth emerges. Rick Hood's left endplate has just collapsed, leaving the springs and roll center height effects to balance the weight transfer to the outside. In this case, the balance is achieved only with lots of push, or understeer, suggesting that most of the roll stiffness is coming from the front end. *Bob Fairman*

Add the endplate and wing effects back in, and equilibrium is achieved with the car loose, or oversteering, implying that the rear tires are experiencing most of the weight transfer. *Bruce Bennett*

mise. One way of fudging the compromise is to install A/R bars. A/R bars permit the use of lower roll centers or softer springs or both. Because they act only to resist the motion of one wheel relative to the other at one end of the car, they do not affect the basic ride quality, and they do not introduce the pitching problem mentioned above. The same rule applies as with springs: If everything else is equal, the end with the stiffer A/R bars will experience the larger share of load transfer.

Chapter 5

Roll Centers and How to Find Them

Recall that part of the load transfer from the inside tires to the outside is carried through the springs, and the remainder is carried through the roll centers. Any difference in the way the load transfer is handled at opposite ends of the car will affect the handling, so we're interested in how the load transfer is distributed from front to rear. If the front takes most of the load transfer, the car will tend to push, or understeer; if the rear takes most of it, the car will tend to be loose—to oversteer.

The part of the load transfer that acts through the springs is split in proportion to the stiffness of the springs at each end. The portion that acts through the roll centers is distributed front to rear according to the roll center heights and the weight distribution at each end. Juggling the heights of the roll centers, then, is one way to tune the chassis to suit the track and the driver's preferences.

Let's look at some common suspension arrangements and see how to locate the roll centers, and how their positions change as the suspension moves. Though independent setups are now starting to appear on open-wheel racers, beam axles remain the most popular arrangement for oval track racers. The position of the roll center on a beam axle suspension is established by whatever linkage locates the axle against sideways movement. Though race cars use very few of the possible ways to locate a beam axle, a lot of different terms refer to basically the same arrangement. The terms used here are those shared by most chassis engineers.

The simplest and most basic way to provide lateral location for an axle is to let a pair of leaf springs do double duty, controlling both up-and-down and sideways motion. Leafs are much stiffer

sideways than they are under vertical loads, so this may be a satisfactory arrangement on a road car. Under racing conditions, though, they still permit a fair bit of lateral movement of the axle, so most racers use a more precise method of axle location. Still, this may be the setup on your tow car or trailer, so it may be worth knowing that the roll center of a leaf-sprung axle is approximately at the height of the spring eyes.

The least expensive, lightest, and simplest form of positive location for a beam axle is a *Panhard rod*—named after the turn-of-the-century French automobile that first used one. This is just a long bar—or tube, usually—running crosswise, jointed to the frame at one end and to the axle at the other.

For all the attraction of its simplicity, a Panhard rod has some problems. First, the axle does

---

James Watt, inventor
of the steam engine, also
invented the Watt's link, which
is just one of many linkages that
provide straight-line motion,
at least over some useful
range of travel.

Though not usually used with a buggy spring, this old modified coupe needs some form of lateral location for the axle because of the divided spring. As Panhard rods go, this is a very short one, which will exaggerate the effects of a changing roll center height and a lateral shift of the axle. *Robin Hartford, Open Wheel Magazine*

not move purely vertically, but rather arcs around the chassis pivot with a radius equal to the length of the rod, so either the axle or the chassis has to shift sideways a bit whenever the axle moves up or down over bumps. Also, if a Panhard rod is used with a leaf spring suspension, the springs try to fight the slight sideways movement, so this combination is seldom seen. This lateral movement can be kept to a minimum by making the Panhard rod as long as possible.

Second, whereas turns in one direction *pull* on the Panhard rod, turns the other way *push* on it, so it has to be made fairly hefty and large in diameter to prevent buckling.

Finally, the roll center with this scheme is located where the centerline of the Panhard rod intersects with the centerline of the car, so it moves somewhat whenever either the axle travels verti-

cally or the car rolls. What is more, it moves downwards with roll in one direction and upwards with roll the other way. For oval racers who use a Panhard rod at the rear, it is usual to mount the right end of the Panhard rod to the chassis, which causes a slight drop in roll center height during left turns, and also ensures that the rod is in tension most of the time.

James Watt, inventor of the steam engine, also invented the Watt's link, which is just one of many linkages that provide straight-line motion, at least over some useful range of travel. Despite the added complication of a Watt's link—it has three times as many pieces as a Panhard rod and five pivots instead of two—it is popular among racers because of its pure straight-line action, and because the roll center doesn't move around when the vehicle rolls. The roll center of a Watt's link is

**The simplest
and most basic way to
provide lateral location for an
axle is to let a pair of leaf springs
do double duty, controlling
both up-and-down and
sideways motion.**

easy to spot: as you might have guessed, it lies right on the center pivot.

Apart from the extra fabricating required, Watt's links involve a couple of points to consider. For one thing, half the linkage lies below the roll center, so there is a limit to how low a roll center you can arrange before you run out of ground clearance. A shorter center link helps in this regard, but it cannot be made too short without limiting the vertical travel. You can easily work out how much travel you have before the path of the center pivot strays off a straight line, by making a simple scale drawing. If you're not keen on drawing, you can mock up the whole thing full size using strips of wood pinned together.

Another point about Watt's links is that they can be used with the center link pivoted on the

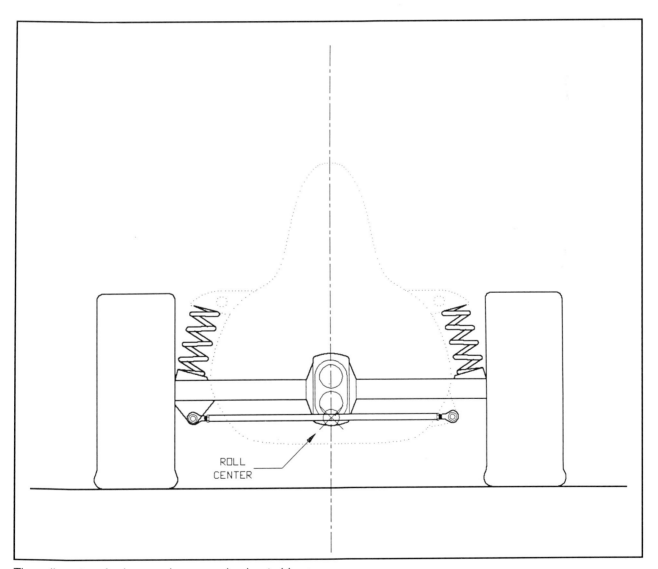

The roll center of a beam axle suspension located by a Panhard rod is at the point where the rod crosses the vehicle centerline.

chassis and the end links jointed to the axle, or the other way around. Most folks do it the other way around, but remember that the roll center is located at the center pivot, so when the car moves up and down on the suspension, the distance between the center of gravity and the roll center keeps changing. Since the portion of the load transfer that is carried through the roll centers depends on the vertical height between the center of gravity (C.G.) and the roll center, variations in this dimension will cause the share of load transfer between front and rear axles to keep changing also—not the best plan for stable, predictable handling. With the center link mounted to the chassis, the roll center remains stationary in relation to the center of gravity.

Back in the forties and fifties when road racing cars in Europe were still using beam axle geome-

try, another popular method of lateral axle location provided this same choice. A peg or roller mounted on the axle center section could be arranged to slide in a slot on the chassis—or the two could be swapped around, with the slot on the axle and the peg on the chassis. Again, the choice was between a roll center that remained at the same height relative to the ground, and one that stayed put relative to the center of gravity.

One other method of locating axles against sideways movement also used in the past by road racers was a giant A-frame mounted crosswise in the chassis, attached to the middle of the axle by a ball joint. The roll center was obviously at the ball joint. Though this setup had the virtue of simplicity, here too the roll center remained stationary with respect to the axle, so it shifted around with

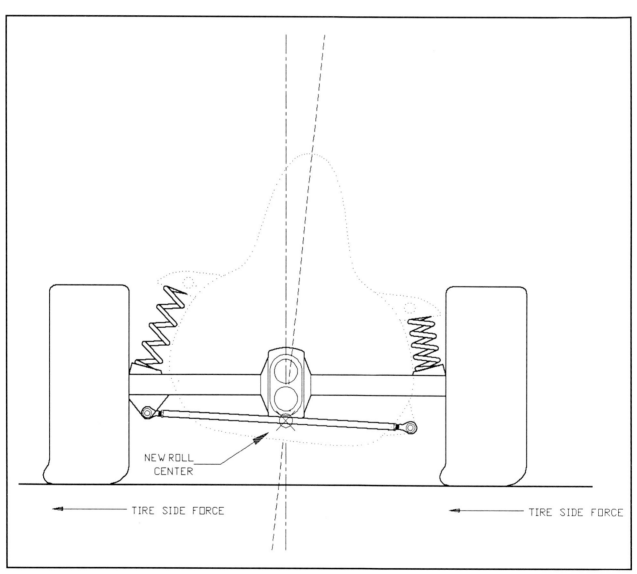

Chassis roll around the roll center causes the Panhard rod to tilt, which repositions the roll center.

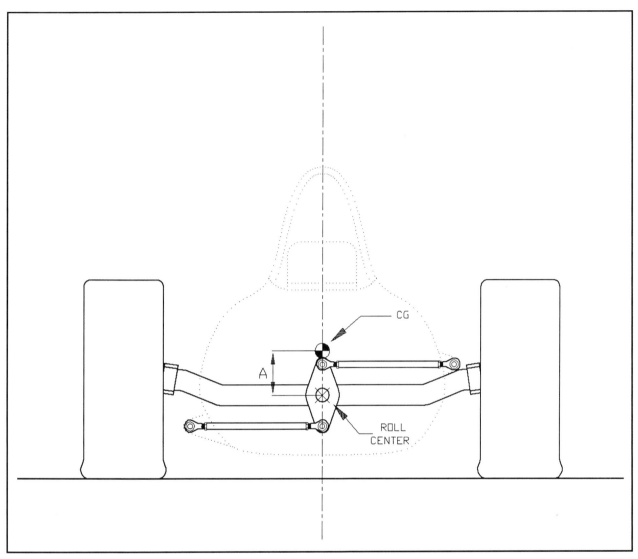

A Watt's link gives pure vertical motion, over a certain range of travel. Though the center pivot is usually mounted on the axle, as shown, it probably should be fixed to the chassis, with the outboard ends of the horizontal links secured to the axle.

respect to the center of gravity whenever the vehicle moved on the suspension.

Though a large number of other possible methods might be used to locate a beam axle—and so define its roll center—almost none of them see common use, so let's turn our attention to independent setups. Again, an infinity of arrangements is possible, but we'll limit our discussion to the types seen on race cars, which means some variation on a double-wishbone system.

We explained in chapter 2 that any system of two links hinged to something solid at one end and to something movable at the other end is—at any given position—equivalent to a single hinged link. The pivot center of this imaginary swing arm lies at the intersection of the lines of the two links, extended until they meet. In other words, the sus-

---

It is important to
realize that the roll center
of a wishbone system moves
whenever the suspension
deflects, whether because
of chassis roll in turns or
because of bumps.

---

pension acts just like a simple swing-axle pivoted at that center. The roll center of such an arrangement lies at the point where a line connecting this imaginary swing-axle pivot to the tire footprint crosses the centerline of the vehicle.

Though most oval racers would shy away from "roll-your-own" independent suspension designs, the initial step in design is simply the reverse of the analysis just described. You decide what roll center height you want, then just draw a line from the tire footprint through the desired roll center, and extend it out some distance. Just how far is another of the many decisions a race car designer has to make. Typical figures are one-and-a-half to three times the car's track width. Lines drawn from this point back to the upper and lower ball joints indicate where the suspension links have to

lie. Of course, that doesn't tell you how *long* the links should be; links of any length lying along these two lines will give exactly the chosen roll center. Varying the lengths of the links will affect how the suspension changes camber as it moves.

Also, it is important to realize that the roll center of a wishbone system moves whenever the suspension deflects, whether because of chassis roll in turns or because of bumps. With a good design, this change will be small, but the designer's problem is to keep the movement of the roll center to a minimum without interfering with the job of controlling camber. For maximum bite, the tire has to be kept square to the track, so the suspension has to camber the tire to cancel the effect of chassis roll in turns.

Obviously, quite a bit of compromise is needed,

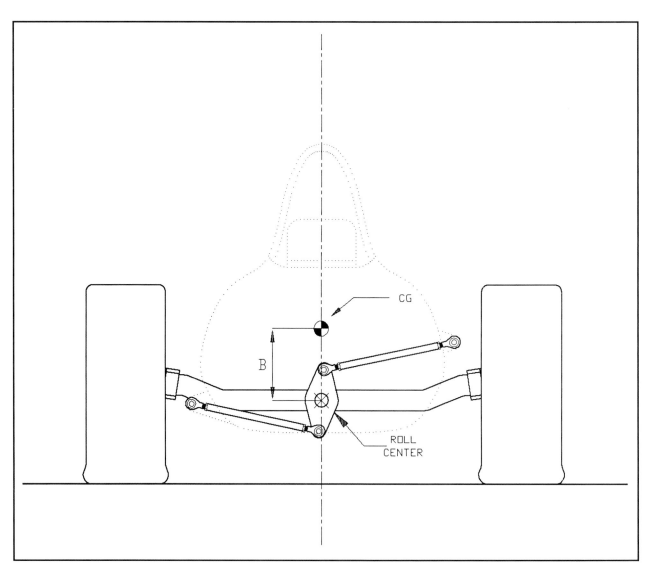

When the Watt's link center pivot is mounted on the axle, vertical movement of the sprung part of the vehicle will change the distance between the roll center and the cen-

ter of gravity. As a result, the fore-aft distribution of roll stiffness will change with bump movement.

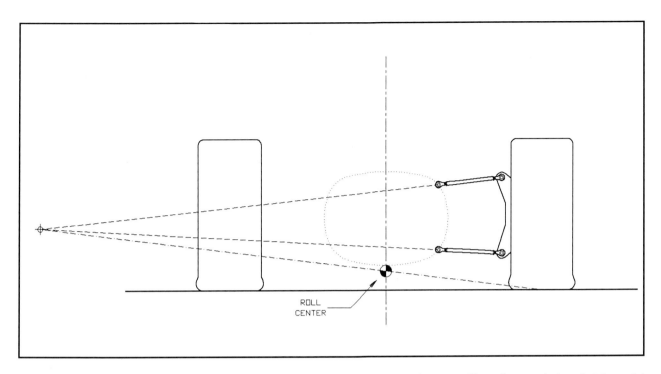

At any given position of the links that make up a double-wishbone independent suspension, the wheel moves as if it were located by a swing-axle pivoted at the point where the link lines intersect. The roll center is found at the point where the imaginary swing-axle crosses the vehicle centerline.

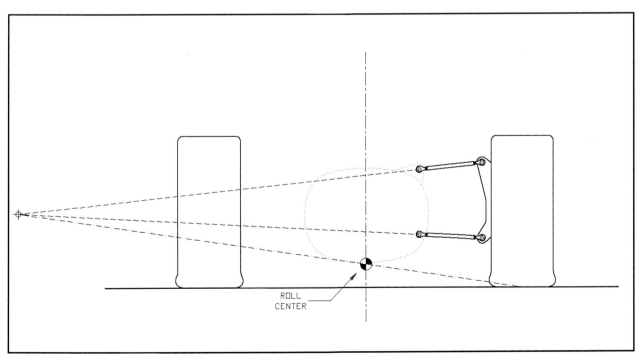

By repositioning the upper and lower ball joints relative to the spindle, it is possible to move the roll center of a wishbone independent suspension without changing the camber geometry of the linkage.

It can't be the idea of an invisible pivot point that accounts for oval track racers' avoidance of independent suspension. A Jacob's ladder, as shown here, is a common replacement for a Panhard rod when space is at a premium.

The long link will move just as if it were pivoted at the point in space where the lines of the two short links intersect. *Robin Hartford, Open Wheel Magazine*

and a satisfactory result is usually arrived at only after a lot of trial and error, either on the drawing board or on the track. This complication is probably a major factor in the slow spread of independent suspension among oval racers, though various computer software packages tailor-made for working through all the variables have become available recently, to take much of the drudgery out of the work.

Once a satisfactory compromise has been reached between camber characteristics and change in roll center height, it is at least possible to change the static roll center height without messing with the other two variables. One approach that has been used by top designers of Formula One and sports cars is to take a pattern of links that is known to give the desired camber change with roll, then to vary the roll center height by moving the entire set of links—relative to the wheel and chassis—without changing their lengths or angles.

Apart from buying or making suspension uprights—maybe you call them "steering knuckles"—that relocate the spindle relative to the upper and lower ball joints, about the only other way to achieve this wholesale relocation of the suspension system is to use wheels or tires of different diameters. Changing wheel sizes obviously involves some complications—getting brakes to fit is just one—and there are limits to how far the roll center can be moved by either of these tricks, anyway. Note that the roll center does not move in proportion to the relocation; it takes a lot of change in the position of the links to achieve a small change in roll center height.

In comparison with beam axles, independent setups have many more potential pitfalls for tuners who tinker with their suspension geometry. Of course, since it is hard to go far wrong with a beam axle, this also means it is equally hard to gain a clear advantage. As we suggested in the introduction, finding more engine power is now both very difficult and very expensive; significant reductions in lap times increasingly have to come from chassis improvements. Despite some resistance, independent suspension will likely continue to make inroads into oval racing for that simple reason.

Chapter 6

Anti-Dive and Anti-Squat

Stiff springs mean large changes in wheel forces in bumpy corners. That hurts handling and also demands a heavy chassis structure to resist the punishment. Soft springs minimize handling disturbances over bumps, and permit lighter construction—or at least give a larger margin of safety for the same weight.

On the other hand, soft springs allow the car to pitch and to roll more. If most of the suspension travel gets used up by this movement, then the car will be more likely to "ground out" or "bottom out" on uneven surfaces. Roll can be controlled by careful planning of roll center heights, which are dealt with in earlier chapters, and through the use of A/R bars, which are talked about in the next chapter. Right now, we're going to deal with the problem of pitch, and how it can be reduced with anti-dive and anti-squat geometry.

When wishbone independent front suspension and soft springs were introduced on passenger cars in the late thirties, and especially after they became widespread in the fifties, the tall sedans of the day tended to drop to their knees whenever the brakes were applied. Some designers dealt with this problem by tilting the pivot axis of both wishbones—when viewed from the side—down toward the front. With this arrangement, any up or down movement of the wheel was accompanied by a certain amount of forward or backward movement.

From the point of view of the chassis, the braking force acts along a line at right angles to the wheel movement path. If the wheel movement were purely vertical, the braking force would act perfectly horizontally—that's what happens when there is no anti-dive. Because this line points

With inboard brakes,
the brake torque reaction is
usually carried into the chassis by
the same route that handles the
axle torque reaction—the one that
tends to lift the pinion nose
during acceleration.

slightly upwards when the links are tilted, however, part of the braking force acts horizontally to slow the car, and part of it acts vertically to prop up the front end.

Though this type of anti-dive geometry can reduce or eliminate pitch under braking, it also creates a couple of problems. First, the forward movement of the wheels that accompanies any upward movement leads to a very harsh ride, which defeats one of the purposes of having soft springs. Second, whereas independent systems can have their steering linkage laid out to minimize unwanted steering effects from bumps, any attempt to use this type of linkage on a beam axle would result in severe bump steer. A bump or dip that affected just one wheel would force the axle to move forwards or backwards at that side, skewing the whole axle sideways in the chassis and so putting a steer angle into both wheels.

With independent suspension, the steering problem can be controlled. Nevertheless, the harsh ride characteristics of this style of anti-dive suspension proved seriously objectionable on passenger cars. The introduction of ball joint suspension in the fifties made a somewhat different scheme possible, in which the upper wishbone is tilted up at the front (or down at the rear, whichever you like), so the tire footprint moves in an arc around the intersection of the lines of the upper and lower wishbones.

Again, the tire footprint moves forwards as it moves up, and the line of action of the brake force again points slightly uphill. As the accompanying illustration in this chapter shows, however, the spindle does not move fore and aft nearly as much as the tire footprint does. This means that when the wheel encounters a bump, the mass of the wheel and tire as a whole is free to move up and over the bump without having to slam "through" it, as in the earlier pattern, though the snubbing of

the forward movement of the contact patch of the tire tends to slow the rotation of the wheel, which adds some ride harshness.

It would be quite possible to adapt this kind of anti-dive linkage to a beam front axle, and if the lengths and angles of the links were carefully chosen, the skewing of the axle on single-wheel bumps could be kept to a minimum. The axis that the wheel swivels around when it is steered is not usually vertical, but rather sloped rearward at the top by a few degrees. This small deviation from vertical, called the *castor* angle, allows the steering to be "self-centering"—the weight of the car acting around the axis of the steering knuckle tends to make the wheels point straight ahead. More castor makes for "heavier" steering; less castor lightens the feel. With either independent suspension or a beam axle, the kind of anti-dive linkage we are describing forces the steering knuckle to rotate somewhat (when viewed from the side) as the wheel moves up or down, so the castor angle is changing all the time. This can result in unpleasant variations in the feel of the steering. Second, in the case of a beam axle, the castor change at one end of the

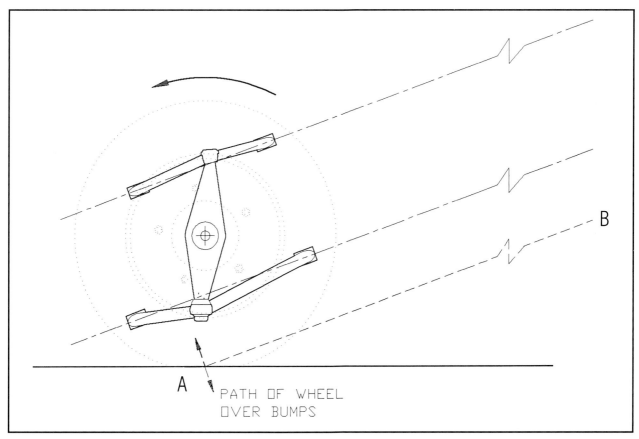

Some passenger and race cars with independent front suspension have tilted their wishbones forwards to gain an anti-dive effect. Because tire forces get fed into the chassis at right angles to the path of wheel travel, the inclined

wheel path means that the braking force acts along the line *A–B*. To the extent that line is pointing upwards, the braking force also acts upwards, which helps counter nose dive under braking.

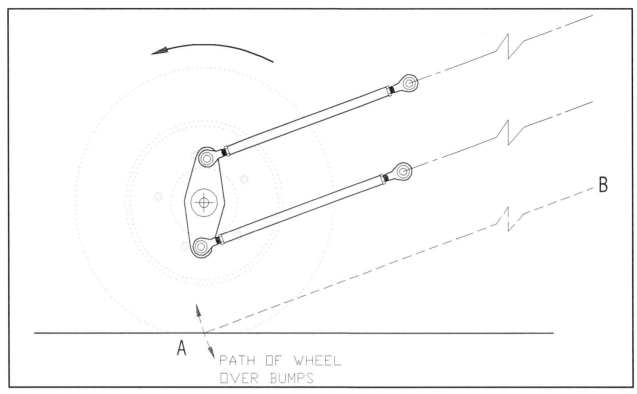

PATH OF WHEEL
OVER BUMPS

A

B

The same principle can also be applied to beam axles; the only thing that matters is that the path of wheel movement—relative to the chassis—is sloped forwards somewhat. On a beam axle, though, a bump affecting just one wheel will result in severe axle steer.

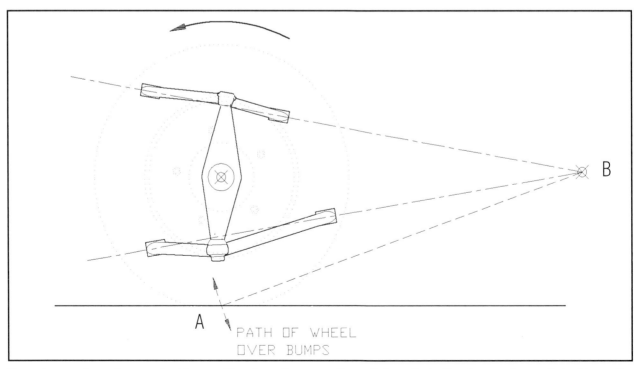

PATH OF WHEEL
OVER BUMPS

A

B

To get away from the rough ride resulting from the arrangements in the previous two illustrations, more modern designs use a geometry of converging link lines to get the anti-dive effect without so much penalty in ride quality. A potential problem is the change in castor angle with wheel movement.

Here's the same thing in real life. Note that the builder has given himself the option of a second bolt hole for the front mounting for the top wishbone. By eyeball, we would guess that the unused hole gives zero anti-dive. *David Allio*

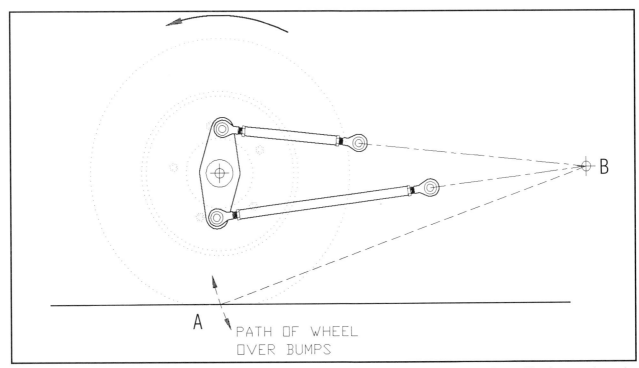

A   PATH OF WHEEL
    OVER BUMPS

Convergent links on a beam axle offer the same combination of anti-dive benefits and acceptable ride quality as the same arrangement on an independent setup. The castor change problem becomes serious with a beam axle: a single-wheel bump or chassis roll in cornering tends to twist the axle.

When wishbone independent front suspension and soft springs were introduced on passenger cars in the late thirties, and especially after they became widespread in the fifties, the tall sedans of the day tended to drop to their knees whenever the brakes were applied.

axle when just that end is deflected will not match up at the opposite end, so the axle tube ends up being twisted.

On bumps that affect only one wheel, this axle twisting will dramatically stiffen the front springs, so again we have reintroduced the very problem we were trying to avoid. And when the car rolls in cornering, the consequences are even worse. Because the axle is very stiff in torsion, it acts as a gi-

gantically stiff A/R bar, which will create a monumental amount of push, or understeer.

The simple fix is to use the illustrated arrangement at just one end of the axle, using a single radius rod at the other end. In that case, however, the upward force acts only at one side of the chassis, so the nose dive will be converted into a sort of diagonal roll toward the unassisted front corner. At first thought, it appears possible to arrange for the reaction force to act nearer the centerline of the car—and so the center of gravity—by mounting the anti-dive linkage at the middle of the axle. Deeper reflection reveals that there is now no easy way to locate the wheels in both the front-rear and left-right directions without bending, twisting, or stretching something.

It might be possible to reduce this geometric "fight" to manageable proportions by mounting some of the links in rubber bushings... on the grounds that an ounce of rubber is worth a ton of theory! Another possible solution to all these problems is to build the axle in two sections with one side spigoted into the other, permitting each side to rotate slightly relative to the other. Or you could forget about dealing with brake torque reactions through a set of links and instead use a torque tube arrangement with a sliding section, like that installed on many oval track rear suspensions.

Ah yes, the rear suspension! Even though anti-dive geometry on the front suspension helps pre-

Here's a clever solution to the axle tube-as-A/R bar problem. This builder has split the axle into two halves, one plugged into the end of the other. The extra link visible be- yond the axle holds the two halves together. *Doug Gore, Open Wheel Magazine*

vent the nose from dropping when the brakes are applied, it does not stop the back end from rising under the same conditions. As you might have guessed, the same basic technique can be used at the back to keep the tail end down. Fortunately, fewer penalties are found here than at the front, and a couple of additional bonuses.

With outboard brakes, almost everything said about the front end can be applied to the back. If the suspension is arranged so that the wheel moves rearwards slightly as it moves up, the line of action of the braking force will be inclined up toward the front, so again, part of the braking force—pulling rearwards—acts horizontally to slow the car and part of it acts vertically downwards to keep the tail down.

Notice, however, that unlike the situation at the front, with anti-dive at the rear, normal up-

ward travel of the suspension over bumps includes a small amount of *rearward* movement. This "compliance" improves the ride, rather than worsening it. This is one of the bonuses of using anti-dive at the back. The other is that it also automatically works the other way around as anti-squat, to keep the back end from dropping under acceleration, because the anti-dive force that acts downwards in braking gets turned into a thrust upwards during acceleration. This anti-squat has nothing to do with the torque reactions of the rear axle; both effects can and do act together.

When inboard brakes are fitted, the situation is a little different. As far as the suspension is concerned, the braking force from the tires now acts through the hub center rather than at the ground, so now we're interested in the path of the hub, not the tire footprint. The same is true even if the brakes are outboard, but the brake torque reaction is carried into the chassis through a separate linkage of some kind. You seldom see this on race cars, but it is quite common on motorcycles.

With inboard brakes, the brake torque reaction is usually carried into the chassis by the same route that handles the axle torque reaction—the one that tends to lift the pinion nose during acceleration. This is likely to be either a torque tube or some kind of torque link, spring loaded or otherwise. In these cases, when the center section is offset to one side, the forces resulting from axle torque reaction will also be offset. A torque tube that runs to the left of the center of gravity will tend to load the left rear, and roll the body to the right, when the power is on. Under braking, the effect will be reversed—unloading the left rear more than the right and tending to make the body roll left.

The application of rear anti-dive–anti-squat is limited by a tire vibration called *chatter* caused by a tendency to unload the tires under braking—the same force that is pulling down on the back of the car is pulling up on the axle. At the front, even using the more modern pattern of links illustrated, experience has shown that the ride can still become unbearably harsh under braking if anti-dive is used to cancel dive completely. General practice, then, is to set the slant of the wishbones or radius

Carried to extremes,
anti-dive can introduce
more problems than it solves.
Applied in small doses, it can permit
a useful reduction in spring rates
without excessive nose dive
when the brakes are on.

rods to provide only some fraction of the full effect. In race cars with independent front suspension, 30-50 percent anti-dive seems to be the practical limit.

To figure the proportion of anti-dive at each end, the first step is to establish what the front-rear brake balance is, then divide the wheelbase in the same proportions. Now the front and rear "lines of action" that we've been talking about are extended until each meets that vertical line. The

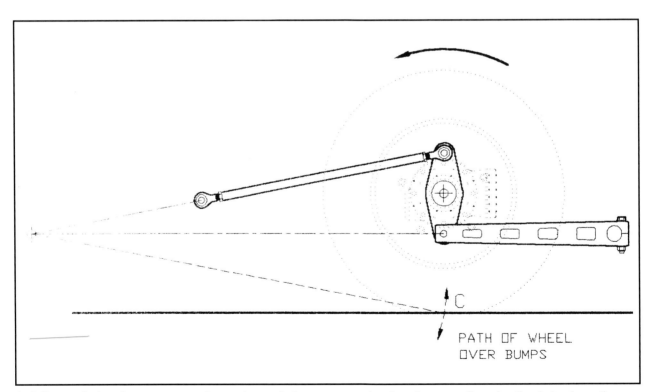

Anti-dive applied to the rear suspension works much the same way as at the front. The braking force pulls along the line C–D, so part of the force acts vertically downwards to keep the tail from rising under braking. When the vehicle is accelerating, the same line of action helps keep the rear end from "squatting," so this arrangement is both anti-dive and anti-squat.

Ah yes, the rear suspension! Even though anti-dive geometry on the front suspension helps prevent the nose from dropping when the brakes are applied, it does not stop the back end from rising under the same conditions. As you might have guessed, the same basic technique can be used at the back to keep the tail end down. Fortunately, fewer penalties are found here than at the front, and a couple of additional bonuses.

With the weight off the axle, this sprinter rear suspension looks all haywire. With the wheel on and the car at normal ride height, though, this setup would closely resemble the one in the previous illustration. *Doug Gore, Open Wheel Magazine*

height of these points above the ground can be compared with the height of the center of gravity. In the accompanying illustration, the intersection point for the line of action of the front suspension is about 82 percent as high as the center of gravity, and the line of action for the rear suspension is about 60 percent of the way up. The front end, then, gives about 82 percent anti-dive and the back about 60 percent, for a total anti-dive effect of about 73 percent. All these figures are way too much for practical use; they are exaggerated to make the principles and the illustrations clearer.

Carried to extremes, anti-dive can introduce more problems than it solves. Applied in small doses, it can permit a useful reduction in spring rates without excessive nose dive when the brakes are on. At the rear, the same geometry reduces tail squat under acceleration and helps plant the rear tires more firmly against the track for a better bite. If you don't get too greedy, and if you take care to avoid excessive axle steer resulting from the use of anti-dive–anti-squat linkage, it is about as close to a free lunch as you're likely to find in race car design.

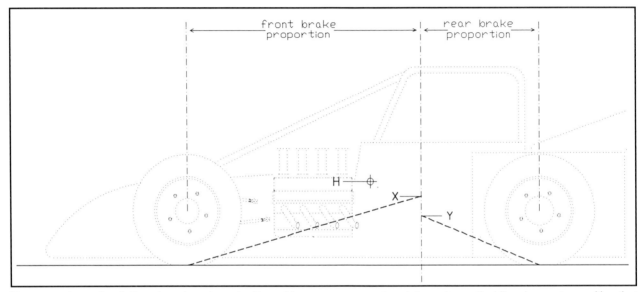

The percentage of anti-dive at each end can be figured by comparing the height of the center of gravity with the heights of the points where the lines of action of the front and rear suspensions intersect a vertical line drawn at a position that represents the front-rear brake force balance. This illustration only applies where outboard brakes are used.

Chapter 7

Anti-roll Bars (Sway Bars) & Dampers (Shock Absorbers)

A/R Bars

It is possible to gain many of the advantages of soft springs, while avoiding the problems of high roll centers, through the use of A/R bars—or sway bars, as they are often called. These simple but effective devices do more than just reduce roll, however.

An A/R bar is nothing more than a torsion bar arranged crosswise in the frame, usually with its ends bent around to form operating levers. (Some applications use separate levers splined onto the ends of the bar.) Each lever arm is connected, usually by a pushrod, to some moving part of the suspension—on independent setups, this is often the upper or lower A-arm. If the car passes over a ridge or rut that affects both wheels on the same axle, both ends of the bar will move up or down the same amount and at the same time, so the bar will just pivot in its mountings and have no effect at all on the suspension.

On the other hand, when the body rolls, the suspension on one side moves up relative to the car while the other side goes down, and this relative movement twists the bar. The bar fights against this twisting with a certain amount of resistance, depending on its length and diameter, and so adds its own contribution to the effort of the springs to keep the car upright.

If an A/R bar is fitted to just one end of the car, the effect when the car rolls will be the same as if stiffer springs had been fitted to that end, and we've already seen in chapter 4 that this will affect the handling of the car by forcing the tires at the stiffer end to carry more of the load transfer that results from cornering. Similarly, if A/R bars are fitted to both ends but they differ in their stiffness,

that too will redistribute the sharing of the load transfer between ends.

The ease with which the resistance to roll, or *roll stiffness*, can be tailored with A/R bars makes this a convenient way to tune the handling. If the car tends to push, or understeer, putting an A/R bar on the rear—or fitting a stiffer one, if one is already there—will force the rear pair of tires to carry more of the load transfer, reducing their collective cornering power and so making the rear end more loose, which is the same thing as reducing

One word of caution:
If the bar is correctly designed
for the "softest" adjustment,
then it may be overstressed in
the "hardest" position.
Depending on the material
and its heat treatment, the bar
may simply snap—in which case,
the symptoms are clear, and
the cure equally obvious.

An anti-roll bar (sometimes called a "sway bar") is a pretty simple piece of equipment—just a bit of bent rod, as seen here, or tubing. To avoid geometric "fight", the bar is usually connected to the suspension via a pushrod with ball-jointed ends. This builder, though, has failed to take advantage of the opportunity to make the A/R bar adjustable. *Doug Gore, Open Wheel Magazine*

the understeer. Similarly, a car that's handling loose will oversteer less if the front A/R bar is stiffened or the rear one softened, because the cornering power of the front pair of tires will then be downgraded compared with that of the rear pair. And all this can be done without changing the basic suspension springs.

The stiffness of an A/R bar is varied by exactly the same means as the effective stiffness of any torsion bar is adjusted: either the bar itself can be swapped for one of a different diameter, or the length of the operating levers can be changed. It's usually easiest to leave the bar alone and work with the levers.

A couple of common methods are used to alter the effective length of the levers. The pushrods

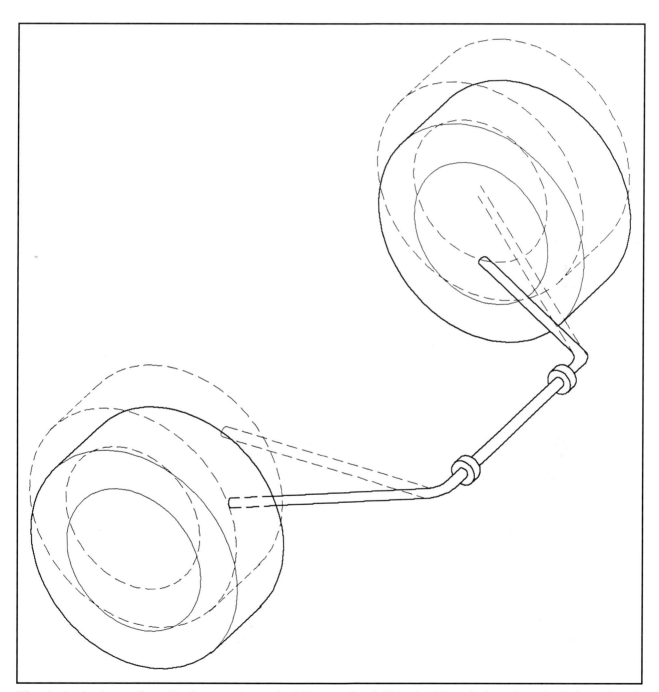

When both wheels are affected by the same bump, the A/R bar just swivels in its mounting bushings. But when the body rolls relative to the wheels, or one wheel moves up and the other one down, the bar is twisted. Like any torsion bar, it "fights back," producing a force that helps resist roll. The same force alters the sharing of roll stiffness between front and rear ends, modifying the balance of the car.

that join the bar to the suspension can be connected by clamps that can be slid to various positions along the bent-over ends of the A/R bar, or the lever arms can have an assortment of holes drilled in them to give a few different fixed positions. With the sliding clamp setup, the adjustment can even be performed from the driver's seat if a push-pull cable is hooked to the movable clamp and run to a lever in the cockpit. The remote linkage can also be hydraulic.

The lever arms themselves will bend a bit whenever the A/R bar is under load, and their deflection will effectively soften the action of the bar. If separate levers are used, they are usually sufficiently robust that their deflection is negligible, but when the levers are formed from the cranked ends of the bar, their bending should be taken into account.

Deliberately making the operating levers flexible, and then taking advantage of that flexibility, gives another—and very slick—way to adjust the A/R bar stiffness. If the lever takes the form of a thin blade, then its stiffness will depend on whether the blade is loaded edge-on or flat-side-on.

By spigoting the blade into a hub in which it can rotate, a continuous range of stiffness can be had, from a maximum when edge-on to a minimum when the blade is loaded across its flat side. Again, it is an easy matter to run a remote control from the adjuster to the driver's seat.

One word of caution: If the bar is correctly designed for the "softest" adjustment, then it may be overstressed in the "hardest" position. Depending on the material and its heat treatment, the bar may simply snap—in which case, the symptoms are clear, and the cure equally obvious. But it is also possible for the bar to yield without breaking, in which case, the handling will change subtly with no obvious cause. Many a chassis developer has been led down the garden path by this kind of near-invisible fault. Painting a pinstripe down the length of the bar when it is new will serve as a "telltale" for this permanent "set." If the bar is yielding, the only fix is either to reduce the stress on the bar by making it longer—but larger in diameter, to keep the rate the same—or to change the material-and-heat treatment combination to

Blade-type operating levers, as shown on this Indy car, are stiff when loaded edge-on, but soft when the flat side is being bent. This provides a convenient method of making running adjustments; note the push-pull cable running to the cockpit. Note, too, how very short the A/R bar itself is—most of the flex in this installation must be coming from the bending of the operating lever, shown here in the stiffest position. *Doug Gore, Open Wheel Magazine*

Though this old Singer midget appears to be fitted with early hydraulic dampers, the friction between the leaves in the transverse buggy spring provides quite a bit of damping itself.

cope with the stress.

As with any torsion bar, the greatest stresses occur in the outer surface—the material in the middle of the bar is hardly stressed at all and is mostly wasted weight. Rifle-drilled torsion bars are available, and the same weight savings can be had in the case of A/R bars by forming them from thick-wall tubing rather than rod stock. Calculating the spring rate of A/R bars is not particularly difficult. Equations for solid and hollow A/R bars are as follows:

Solid Steel Bars

$$\text{Rate (lb/in)} = \frac{1,1,000,000 \times D^4}{L \times l^2}$$

Hollow Steel Bars

$$\text{Rate (lb/in)} = \frac{1,100,000 \times (D^4 - d^4)}{(L \times l^2)}$$

Variables for both equations are as follows:
D = outside diameter of bar, in inches
d = inside diameter of bar, in inches
L = length of torsion bar, in inches
l = length of lever arm, in inches

A little thought will reveal that on bumps that affect just one wheel, the A/R bar will add its rate to that of the basic road springs, stiffening the ride. Now, comfort doesn't mean much in racing, but the arguments against stiff springs remain. For passenger car work, it is generally agreed that the single-wheel rate contributed by the A/R bar should not exceed 50 percent of the basic spring rate. Racers can doubtless tolerate a larger figure than that, but remember that one purpose of A/R bars is to permit the use of softer springs, for all the reasons set out in chapter 3.

Note, too, that the relationship between the force at the wheel due to the spring–A/R bar combination and the force due to the shock absorber will change depending on whether just one wheel or both are affected. If the shock absorber is well matched to the springing on a bump that affects both wheels—one that doesn't involve the A/R bar action—then it will be too soft on single-wheel bumps where the A/R bar takes part, and vice versa. For all these reasons, if the A/R bar adds a wheel rate over single-wheel bumps that much ex-

ceeds the 50 percent figure, then maybe the basic springs are too soft, or the roll centers too low.

Shock Absorbers, Or Dampers

Let's get one thing straight: shock absorbers don't absorb shocks. Their main purpose is to smother, or damp, unwanted vibrations of the springs, and that's the reason they are called dampers through most of the world outside North America.

Recall that springs trade force for distance. If a spring is loaded with a weight, it will be compressed a certain distance, and in response to that displacement, it will push back with a force matching the weight. If the spring is momentarily compressed further, and then suddenly released, the extra energy temporarily stored in the spring will accelerate the weight back up with a force that depends on how far the spring was compressed beyond the rest position. That accelerating force will fade away to nothing as the weight rises to its rest position, but at that point, the weight will have a certain upward speed, so it will overshoot the original rest position, further relaxing the spring.

Eventually, the weight will "run out of gas," since gravity is sucking it down and the spring is no longer pushing it up. At that point, we have a weight poised over a relaxed spring, so the weight will start down again. When the weight reaches its rest position, the spring force will match the force of gravity acting on the weight, but again the weight has a certain velocity that has to be arrested, so it will again overshoot the rest position. This would go on forever if it were not for some slight aerodynamic drag, plus a certain amount of internal molecular friction within the material of the spring. In practice, with metal springs, it will take many, many cycles of this trading back and forth of stored energy in the spring and inertial energy in the bouncing weight before the system comes to a halt.

Clearly, without some sort of friction applied to the system, a single bump that compresses the springs beyond their rest position and then, a moment later, relaxes them will cause the car and wheels to "pogo" almost indefinitely. The purpose, then, of the shock absorbers (uh, sorry, dampers) is to provide the friction that's needed to snub the extra cycles, by converting into heat the *kinetic energy* (the energy of motion) contained in the bouncing weight.

In the early days, when leaf springs were used at all four corners on both road and race cars, the sliding friction between the moving leaves provid-

Left
Because interleaf friction is unpredictable at best, separate friction dampers were adopted very early in race car history. Tightening the nut on the star-shaped spring washer permits adjustment of the damping force. *Bob Fairman*

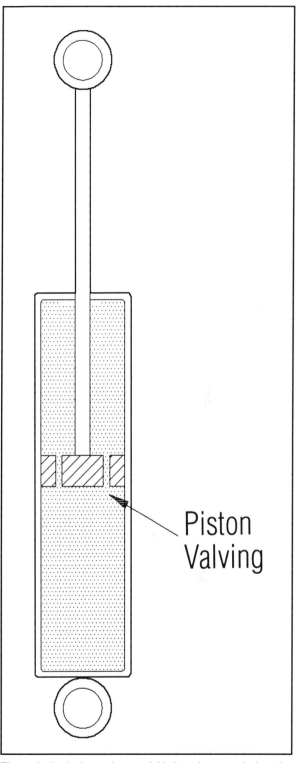

Piston Valving

The velocity independence of friction dampers led to the introduction of hydraulic "flit-gun" shocks in the late twenties, shown schematically here. The hydraulic oil's resistance to flowing through the piston orifices provides a damping force that depends strongly on velocity. The volume occupied by the piston rod changes according to the position of the piston, however, so the simple arrangement shown here won't work.

ed a fair degree of damping by itself. Later, friction dampers—sometimes called "scissors shocks"—were introduced, which worked on the same physical principle but at least had the advantage that the friction force was more predictable, and could be adjusted.

This kind of friction damping has a couple of drawbacks, though. First, the "stiction" between the moving surfaces means that small forces will have no effect—the suspension will basically be locked solid over small disturbances, and a significant amount of force needs to be applied before any springing action occurs at all. Once the system is broken loose, a second problem becomes apparent: the friction force does not vary with the speed of sliding. Fast movements get damped with the

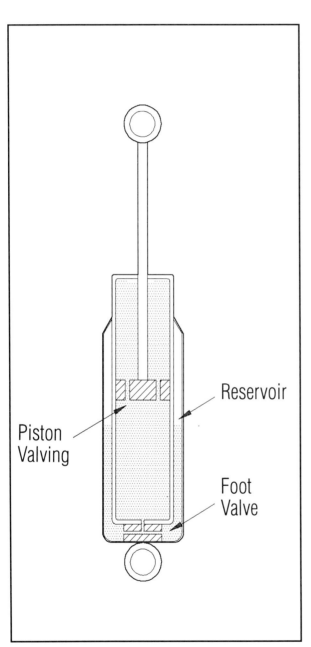

Piston Valving

Reservoir

Foot Valve

To compensate for the constantly changing volume occupied by the piston rod, the double-tube type of dampers used on most passenger cars employ a separate reservoir wrapped around the outside of the working cylinder. The foot valve at the base of the working cylinder contributes something to the bump damping but allows free flow on rebound.

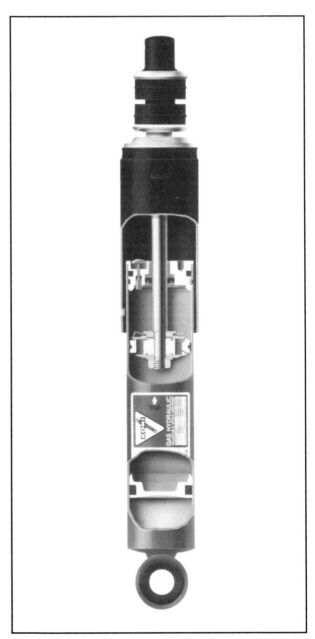

The best modern dampers, for both street and track, are of the monotube or high-pressure type. Compensation for the piston rod volume is achieved by the gas chamber visible at the bottom of this cutaway Koni shock. A floating piston, also visible, separates the high-pressure gas from the hydraulic fluid. Foaming, or aeration, is greatly reduced by the complete isolation of the fluid from the air. *Koni America*

same force as slow ones.

Some modern materials such as Teflon—du Pont's trade name for tetrafluoroethylene, or TFE, the nonstick plastic used on frying pans—show very little difference between their static and dynamic friction characteristics. In other words, the amount of force needed to break the surfaces loose is virtually the same as the friction force when the surfaces are sliding. A friction damper using this type of material largely overcomes the stiction problem of friction dampers. Unfortunately, nothing can be done about the second problem—the force remaining constant, whatever the speed of the moving parts. Mostly for this reason, the form of damper used universally for nearly half a century has been the familiar hydraulic type, and, apart from an occasional appearance on the front end of dragsters, friction dampers are now found only in museums.

The basic principle behind hydraulic dampers is dead simple: A piston with holes in it is fitted into a cylinder filled with oil. As the piston strokes in or out of the cylinder, the oil is forced to flow through the holes. The resistance of the oil to being squeezed through these tiny orifices creates the friction force that provides the damping.

This simplified damper has one snag, however:

it won't work! As the piston moves farther into the cylinder, the volume below it gets smaller and the volume above gets bigger, but the increase above is less than the decrease below because some of the volume above the piston is getting occupied by the piston rod as more of it enters the cylinder. If you were to succeed in forcing the piston into the cylinder, and no leaks occurred, the whole business would soon explode!

The most common solution to this problem is to provide a reservoir outside the working cylinder to accommodate the excess oil. With this arrangement, some sort of restricting valve needs to be inserted between the base, or foot, of the working cylinder and the reservoir, to avoid the risk of cre-

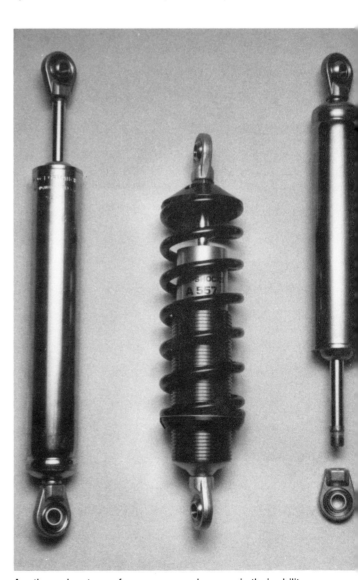

Another advantage of gas pressure dampers is their ability to work upside-down. That means the heavier cylinder can be mounted to the chassis, and the lighter piston rod can be attached to the suspension, slightly reducing unsprung weight. *Doug Gore, Open Wheel Magazine*

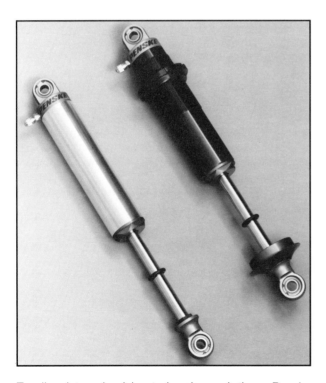

To allow internal valving to be changed, these Penske racing dampers are completely rebuildable. Because dismantling would cause loss of the high-pressure gas in the compensating chamber, a Schraeder (tire) valve is provided for recharging the gas. Robin Hartford, Open Wheel Magazine

A little thought will reveal that on bumps that affect just one wheel, the A/R bar will add its rate to that of the basic road springs, stiffening the ride.

ating a partial vacuum above the piston and sucking air past the rod seal as the piston moves in. This valve, however, has to permit oil to flow easily back into the cylinder on the out stroke.

The foot valve's restriction to flow into the reservoir on the compression stroke automatically provides some degree of damping of bump travel, and some dampers have been built that get all their bump damping this way. The volume of oil expelled to the reservoir—exactly equal to the volume of piston rod that has entered the cylinder—is small in comparison with the volume of flow through the piston. For that reason, it is more usual for the bump damping to be shared between the foot valve and the piston. Because the foot valve offers negligible restriction to flow in the opposite direction, all the damping on the extension stroke—corresponding to rebound travel—must be provided by the orifices and valves in the piston.

A drawback to conventional "double-tube" damper construction is the presence of an airspace above the oil in the reservoir. The violent agitation due to wheel movement, combined with the heating and turbulence of the oil flowing through the various valves and orifices, can cause the oil to mix with some of this air and so *aerate*, or foam. The sudsy emulsion that results offers much less resistance to flow than liquid oil, and is also compressible.

To tackle the problem of aeration, some high-quality dampers use a donut-shaped rubber bladder inflated with a gas—usually Freon—to fill the space above the oil in the reservoir. This bladder, easily squeezed smaller to allow oil to flow into the reservoir, isolates the oil from contact with air, reducing aeration. The constant pressure applied to the oil by the bladder also helps inhibit the formation of bubbles within the oil.

Another alternative to the double-tube damper is single-tube construction. Here, the volume of the piston rod is compensated by a volume of compressible gas—often nitrogen—at the end of the working cylinder. A "floating" piston is usually, though not always, used to separate the oil from the gas. Even without a separating piston, the relatively high pressure of the trapped gas helps sup-

press the formation of bubbles within the hydraulic oil. Most top-quality racing dampers are of the single-tube type; about their only drawback is the extra length needed to contain the gas chamber and floating piston.

The pressure that builds up when a fluid is forced through an orifice depends on the square of the velocity of the flow—double the flow rate means four times the pressure. Since the pressure in the fluid acting against the piston produces the damping force, a damper constructed as described here will exert a damping force proportional to the square of the speed of movement. Whereas a friction damper provides too little force to cope with high-speed movements, this simplified hydraulic damper will provide too much. What's actually wanted is a damping force that increases more or less in direct proportion to the speed. To achieve that characteristic, hydraulic dampers are fitted with *blow-off valves* that open progressively as the pressure across them rises, reducing the restriction of the orifices.

If all the oil had to pass through the blow-off valves—or "ride-control valves," as they are called—we would have the same problem as with a friction damper: the system would remain locked solid for small force inputs, until enough pressure was developed to crack the valves off their seat. For that reason, the flow restriction for slow movements is provided by a leak path consisting partly of leakage past the piston seal and partly of flow through orifices in the piston or foot valve or both. With the right design, the basic "square law" increase in force as speed rises can be modified to give a force that comes very close to being in direct proportion to the speed.

The right ratio between bump damping and rebound damping is a matter of considerable dispute, and depends partly on the kind of track the car is operating on, partly on details of the car's suspension system, and partly on driver's preference. To increase ride comfort, most of the damping in passenger car applications takes place on rebound—a 30:70 ratio of bump damping force to rebound damping force is typical.

Though this reduces the vertical force fed into the car when a wheel hits a bump, a series of closely spaced bumps can present a problem. The wheel can move upward over the first bump with little resistance, but the strong rebound damping slows the recovery to normal ride height. If a number of additional bumps follow in rapid succession, the car gets closer and closer to the ground as the suspension "pumps down." Partly for this reason, some racing shocks offer something closer to 50:50 damping. Even though this may be desirable—indeed necessary—on bumpy dirt tracks, many high-quality dampers intended for use on paved tracks maintain a ratio of bump-to-rebound damping clos-

We can only hope that both the dampers on the rear of Bo Rawdon's modified are of the gas pressure type. Conventional double-tube dampers would soon get air and oil mixed in a lay-down installation like this, and foam doesn't work well as a damping medium. *David Allio*

er to the 30:70 of passenger car applications.

Another reason for designing in more bump damping, even though it acts to stiffen the suspension—which, we keep arguing, is a bad thing—is to control the motion of the wheel and tire relative to the car, as opposed to the movement of the car relative to the wheels. Despite the use of lightweight suspension components, race cars typically have a higher ratio of unsprung-to-sprung weight than do road cars, so need proportionally more damping force to control the tendency of their moving unsprung components to "overshoot."

In this connection, keep in mind that the velocity of the wheels moving over bumps is much higher than the velocity of the car bouncing or rolling on the springs. The control of wheel motion, then, involves the damper characteristic at high stroking speeds, whereas body motion is controlled by the dampers' low-speed properties.

The resistance that the dampers offer to the relatively low-speed movement of the car on its suspension can significantly affect the handling of the car during the transition from straight running to turning, and vice versa. Assuming the

track is smooth, and ignoring aerodynamic effects, once the car has settled into a turn and has achieved steady-state cornering, the distribution of vertical loading on the tires will be completely accounted for by the characteristics of the springs and A/R bars, and by the height of the roll centers. The dampers have nothing whatever to do with the balance of the car under these steady-state conditions.

But during the transition period, the car rolls in response to the growing side forces, and the dampers will resist that roll just the same as if it were a gradual upward movement of the outboard wheels—say, over a gradual, shelving ramp. During this transitional rolling phase, the force fed into the car, and reflected to the tires at the other end of the spring–damper–A/R bar combination, will depend strongly on the forces the dampers develop in this low-speed regime.

If the front dampers offer more resistance than the rears during this phase of corner entry, more of the load transfer will be carried by the front, so the car will tend to push. As a steady-state turn is approached, though, the effect of the dampers will

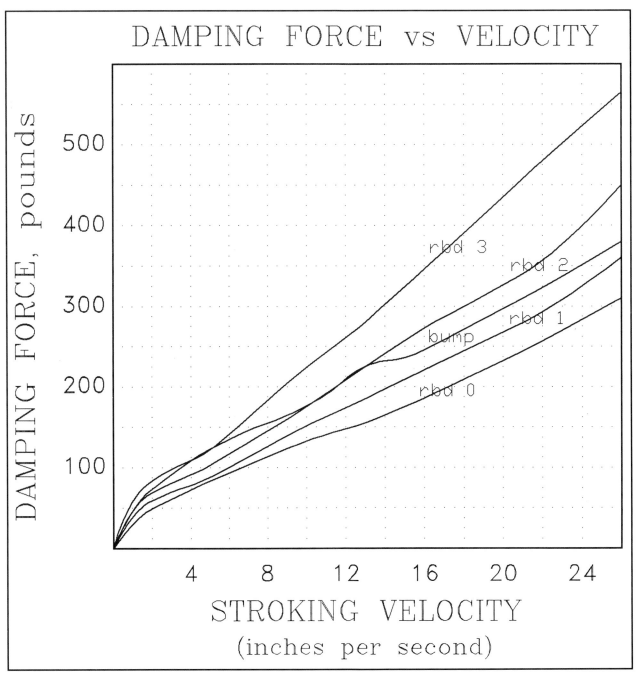

DAMPING FORCE vs VELOCITY

DAMPING FORCE, pounds

500

400

300

200

100

rbd 3

rbd 2

rbd 1

bump

rbd 0

4   8   12   16   20   24

STROKING VELOCITY

(inches per second)

Some racing shocks are adjustable only by swapping internal parts, but Koni, among others, provides external adjustment. Though bump damping is fixed, rebound can be adjusted in four steps, from somewhat less than the bump force to something close to 70:30. Note how close this damper comes to providing a damping force that is proportional to piston velocity.

dwindle away, and the car will revert to a looser posture—either understeering less or oversteering more. This can complicate the driver's task: the car tends to turn in reluctantly, then begins to get more tail happy. The opposite effect—more resistance to movement in roll at the rear—will mean that the rear pair of tires carries more of the load transfer during the beginning of the turning ma-

neuver, making the car loose. As the roll settles down to a steady value, this oversteering tendency will decrease. Depending on the setup of the car and the driver's preference, this "twitchy" initial response can make the car turn in faster, and the gradual increase in understeer (or reduction in oversteer) can make it easier to pick an accurate line through the turn.

Chapter 8

Turning Left, Naturally

Remember the old gag about putting bigger tires on the rear so the car will always be "running downhill"? No one over the age of ten takes that seriously, of course, but for a locked axle car that only turns left, putting a bigger tire on the right rear wheel does make sense—it seems natural and obvious that a car without a differential will tend to turn towards whichever rear tire is smaller. The issue is much more complex than that, however. First, understand that stagger, which is what we call using two different size tires, is a solution to a basic problem with locked axles—a strong tendency to run straight and to resist turning, either left or right. And locked axles themselves are a solution to another problem—the torque reaction of a live axle that tries to pick up the right rear tire. If a differential is fitted, that unloaded right rear tends to spin; a locked axle solves that problem, but introduces a new one—the "push" that results when both drive wheels are forced to rotate in unison. Stagger converts this relentless straight ahead preference of the car into an equally strong inclination to run in a circle of a specific radius. But, as if to prove once again that the main source of problems is solutions, stagger introduces difficulties of its own. For one thing, the same stagger that helps when turning left hurts when going straight—usually thought of as the drag of the smaller tire directly fighting the efforts of the larger one to propel the car.

We've worked out some numbers for an imaginary 1,580lb vehicle, with 57 percent of its weight on the rear axle and 55 percent left side weight (about 495lb on the left rear, 405lb on the right rear), a 30in diameter left rear tire and 4.7in of

There's another effect of stagger that we should mention. Running a smaller tire on one side will obviously tilt the entire axle down toward the smaller tire. That means that both tires will be running with a small—but significant—amount of camber.

stagger. Under these conditions, the tire fight would consume a mere 3.5 horsepower at a steady 60mph!

There is a larger source of drag, though, that is related to the "crabbing" of the car. To keep the vehicle going straight, the front tires have to provide a force pointed to the right, and they create drag as a result. Just how hard the front tires have to shove to the right depends on the left-turning torque created around the mass center of the car by the imbalance between the forces at the rear tires. This "stagger torque," as we will call it, depends in turn on the track width and wheelbase of the car, the weight distribution, and on the amount of stagger.

What we've labeled as "stagger torque" in the accompanying illustration is created by the tire forces, marked F-right side and F-left side. What can we say about the sizes of these individual forces?

Consider what happens when two tires of different diameters are connected together by a "live" (rotating) axle, and then are forced to roll in a

straight line. Let's imagine, too, that no torque is being applied to the axle by either the engine or the brakes, as if the car is coasting, or being towed. We've chosen this situation to simplify the first steps in our analysis, but it is not completely unrealistic. It can occur, briefly, twice a lap, just as the driver is lifting off the throttle.

In this situation, the tires are obviously fight-

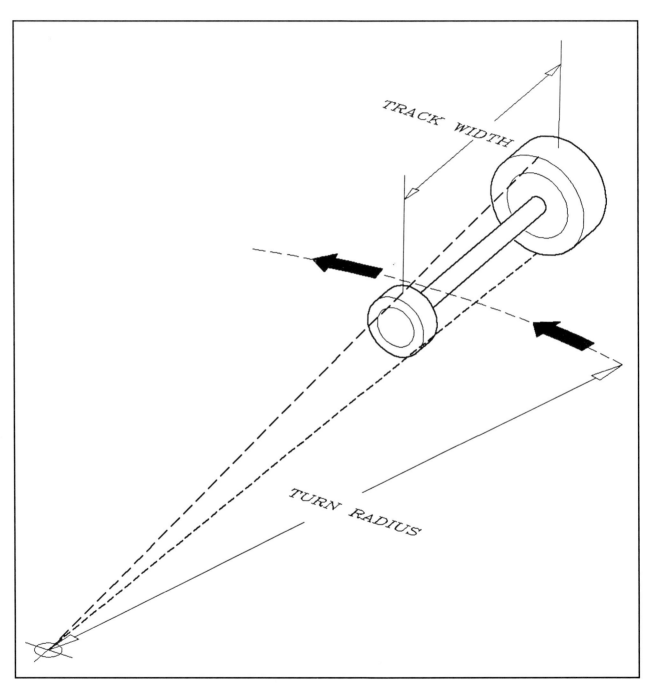

When an axle has a small tire on one side and a large one on the other, it will naturally roll in a circular path. The radius of that path will depend on the difference in tire sizes—the amount of stagger—and on the track width. For

instance, 10 percent stagger on a track width of 5ft will give a natural "tracking" radius of 50ft; 5 percent stagger will give a radius of 100ft.

ing each other; the question is, which one will win? You might figure that the bigger tire will dominate, or maybe the more heavily loaded tire—whichever side it's on—will "hook-up" and drag the other one along at the same speed. But consider what happens when a tire is forced to run a little faster or slower than the ground is passing by.

In fact, every tire slips slightly whenever it is called on to produce a force acting forward or rearward. We're talking just a few percent here—this slight amount of creep is not the same thing as tire-smoking wheelspin, but it's important to realize that a tire cannot produce any force to accelerate (or slow) the car unless it is running at least a bit faster (or slower) than the road is going by. What's more, the fore-aft force a tire can develop depends on the amount of slip, expressed as a percentage. (For instance, if the tire is going 110mph while the car is going 100mph, the tire has 10 percent slip.) The relationship between slip and the longitudinal force the tire produces is shown in the first accompanying graph.

Of course, the fore-aft force from the tire also depends on the vertical force pressing the tire onto the ground. To enable us to see the pattern without having to keep specifying these forces in pounds, several of the accompanying graphs and illustrations refer to the "longitudinal force coeffi-

cient." This is just the ratio between the vertical force and the amount of longitudinal force the tire can supply. From the second graph, for example, we see that this particular tire at 20 percent slip has a coefficient of about 1.7. That means it will push the car forward with 1.7 times the force pressing it on the ground. If that vertical force is, say, 500lb, the horizontal force will be 1.7 times 500lb—or 850lb.

For one thing, the same stagger that helps when turning left hurts when going straight—usually thought of as the drag of the smaller tire directly fighting the efforts of the larger one to propel the car.

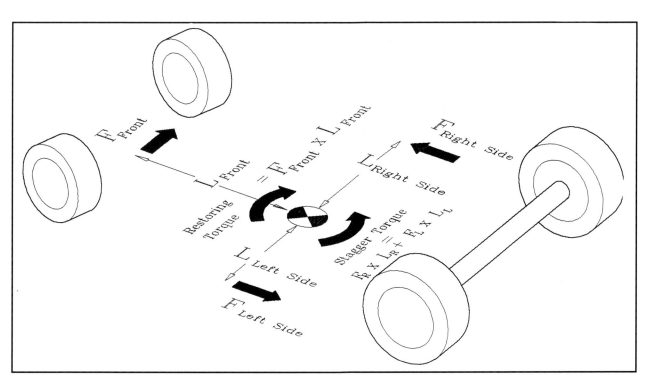

Under coasting and light throttle, the longitudinal tire force from the left rear is acting backwards, creating a counterclockwise torque around the car's center of gravity. Meanwhile, the right rear's force acts forwards, adding a further counterclockwise torque. When the left rear is driving, the torque resulting from its longitudinal force reverses, tending to reduce the total "stagger torque." Still, under most conditions, an imbalance will exist between the separate torques. In all cases, the front tires have to provide the restoring torque for the car to go straight.

At first, a small increase in slip gives a proportional increase in the coefficient, but then the curve peaks and starts to drop off again. At the top of the curve the tire is giving its best performance—that's where the driver would try to hold the tires to get maximum acceleration. In our example, the coefficient reaches its maximum value of about 2.0 (marked on the graph with an "X") when the tire is slipping at about 7 percent. Beyond that point, it's all smoke and not much poke—more slip actually produces less forward (or rearward) thrust.

Now let's return to our imaginary race car, still being towed in a straight line. We've said that the right rear tire is 4.7in bigger in circumference than the left rear, which is a 5 percent difference on a 30in O.D. tire. We also know that this 5 percent stagger will force one or both tires to slip, but we don't know how the total of 5 percent slip is divided up between the tires. We do know, however, that the tires are connected together by a common axle, and that the battle between them will produce a torque in that axle.

Now, here's the key: there can only be one val-

What's more, the fore-aft force a tire can develop depends on the amount of slip, expressed as a percentage. For instance, if the tire is going 110mph while the car is going 100mph, the tire has 10 percent slip.

On short tracks with tight turns, the amount of stagger can become awesome. The stagger of these tires isn't as extreme as some. *Doug Gore, Open Wheel Magazine*

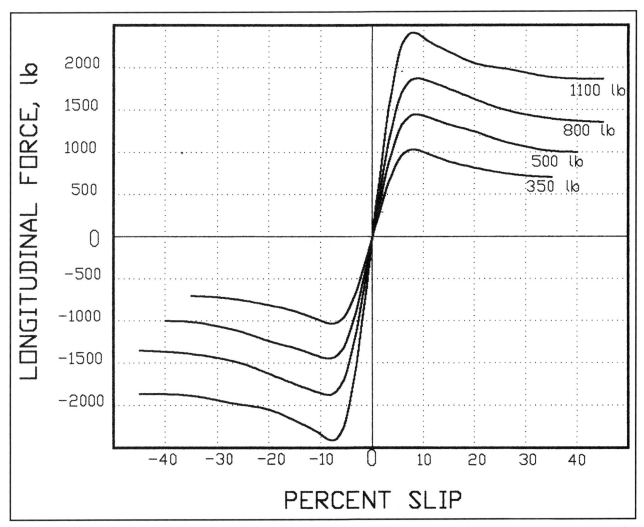

In the same way that the side force produced by a tire depends on the tire's slip angle, a tire's ability to produce a longitudinal force depends on how much it slips in the fore-aft direction. In small amounts, this slippage is best described as "creep"; true slipping of the rubber over the ground probably doesn't start until the straight-line part of the curve starts to bend over toward the horizontal.

ue for that torque, and it must be the same at both ends. Because the right rear tire is larger in diameter than the left, it gets a little more leverage on the axle—5 percent more, in fact—so it will take a 5 percent greater force at the tread rubber of the smaller left side tire to match the opposing torque of the larger right side tire. In other words, the ratio of the longitudinal forces between the two tires must be 1.05 to 1. We know the vertical force clamping each tire onto the ground, so we can figure out the ratio between the coefficients in effect at each tire.

We also know that the total amount of slip is 5 percent, no matter how it is divided up between tires. At this point, we could come up with two coefficients that have the right ratio between them and which correspond to a total of 5 percent slip. If you went through that exercise for the example we have

created, you would discover that the right rear is slipping (in the forward direction) a bit less than 2.7 percent, and the left rear is slipping (in the rearward direction) a little more than 2.3 percent.

So far all we've done is figure out how the slippage that accompanies stagger is distributed between the tires, under the somewhat artificial condition of coasting. By itself, that doesn't mean much. But imagine adding just a little engine torque to help whatever is "towing" our imaginary racer.

The right rear, already slipping in the forward (i.e. driving) direction, will start to slip more, while the left rear, which is dragging rearward, will slip less. If we gradually add more throttle, we will obviously reach the point where the left rear is rolling at exactly road speed, while all the slip—5 percent in our example—is happening at the right

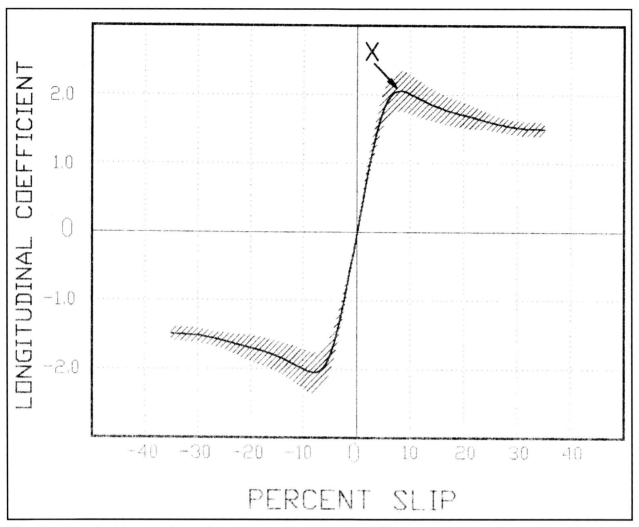

When the longitudinal forces in the previous graph are divided by the normal (vertical) force clamping the tire on the track, the result is a plot of longitudinal force coefficient versus slip. Though an underloaded tire works better, the variation in coefficient at different loads is comparatively small—all the separate plots in the previous graph lie within the shaded area. With stagger, each tire will be operating at a different point on the curve. Changes in slip rate will move both tires the same left-right distance across this graph, since the difference between them will remain constant, equal to the percent of stagger.

rear. The left rear is now essentially free-rolling. Because it is slipping neither forward nor backward, it can exert no longitudinal force at all against the car—all the force, and thus all the stagger torque, is being produced by the right rear. This is truly "driving off the right rear."

If we now add just a smidgen more torque, both tires will start slipping in the forward direction, and the right rear will always be slipping 5 percent more than the left, as long as the car is going straight. To reach this point, though, the right rear must have reached or passed the peak of the slip/thrust curve, so while the left rear is coming on like gangbusters, the right rear is losing ground. This produces the odd result that the torque tending to twist the car to the left starts to diminish as the torque driving the axle is increased.

Theory, and the accompanying graph, suggest that the stagger torque would eventually fade to nothing (and apparently even begin to reverse), if the car could be kept pointed straight while accelerating violently. However, because the right rear will be way past its optimum slip rate by the time the left side is slipping 4 percent or 5 percent, the range of slip experienced in actual racing use on pavement probably ensures that the stagger torque is always positive.

There are several factors confusing the issue, though. First, under hard acceleration the front end will get light from weight transfer, so the ability of the front tires to provide a force opposing the

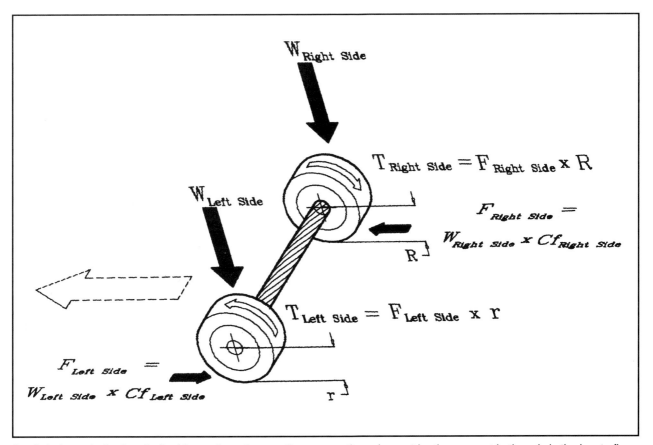

$$T_{\text{Right Side}} = F_{\text{Right Side}} \times R$$

$$F_{\text{Right Side}} = W_{\text{Right Side}} \times Cf_{\text{Right Side}}$$

$$T_{\text{Left Side}} = F_{\text{Left Side}} \times r$$

$$F_{\text{Left Side}} = W_{\text{Left Side}} \times Cf_{\text{Left Side}}$$

Any imbalance in the longitudinal forces from the rear tires will tend to twist the axle. Recognizing that the torque in the axle must be the same at both ends is the key to figuring the slip rate for individual wheels.

In fact, every tire slips slightly whenever it is called on to produce a force acting forward or rearward. We're talking just a few percent here—this slight amount of creep is not the same thing as tire-smoking wheelspin, but it's important to realize that a tire cannot produce any force to accelerate (or slow) the car unless it is running at least a bit faster (or slower) than the road is going by.

leftward bias will diminish in proportion. Since the lateral force the front tires can develop depends (in the same way that their longitudinal force does) on the vertical force holding them on the ground, then the driver's experience will be that the amount of right-hand steering he has to dial in will be little affected by applying power. Drivers' experiences differ in this matter—some say more throttle increases the left turning tendency; others seem to experience what the theory suggests.

Now let's look at what happens with the same theoretical racer when it is in a turn. If the radius of that turn "matches" the amount of stagger, there will be no fight between the tires—any longitudinal slip will take place equally at both of them, as on a locked axle car *without* stagger running in a straight line. At the same time, because the car is turning, there will be weight transfer from the inside to the outside, in proportion to how fast the car is going around the corner.

If our imaginary car is cornering hard—say about 45mph in a turn of 100ft radius, and if the center of gravity is 16in above the ground (a reasonable figure), then enough load will be transferred to the right rear to raise the force clamping it on the track from 405lb when going straight to

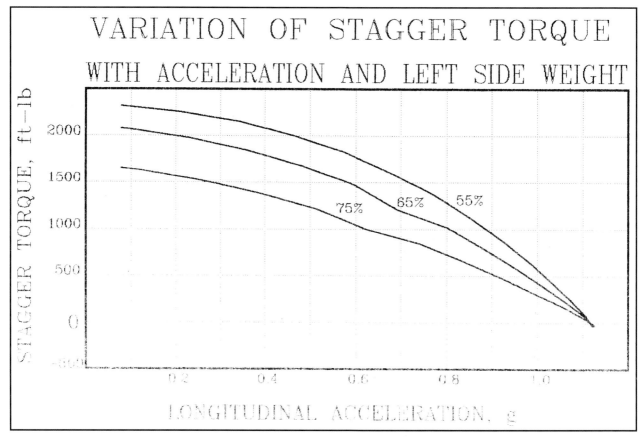

VARIATION OF STAGGER TORQUE
WITH ACCELERATION AND LEFT SIDE WEIGHT

Though the effect may be masked from the driver by the unloading of the steered front wheels during acceleration, calculation suggests that the stagger torque becomes smaller as more power is transmitted. And, paradoxically, the greater the amount of left-side weight, the less the stagger torque.

582lb. That increase in vertical loading on the right rear means that, at a given slip rate, the vertical force will now produce a much larger left-turning torque around the mass center. (It's important to realize that the mass center hasn't moved—it's still 3in left of the vehicle centerline.) Meanwhile, at the same slip rate, the opposite acting torque produced by the thrust of the left rear will be smaller, because that tire's vertical force has dropped by the same 177lb that got added to the right side.

Alas, the situation grows hopelessly complicated at this point because a tire's longitudinal coefficient also depends strongly on whether the tire is being asked to develop any lateral (sideways) force. And that variation is by no means linear. Nevertheless, we can predict that if the weight transfer due to cornering is less than the static difference in side-to-side weight, the imbalance in forward thrusts from the tires will tend to cause understeer; if the weight transfer exceeds the static difference, then the car will tend to oversteer. A balanced condition—neutral steer—will occur only when the weight transfer exactly cancels the static left side bias.

If this balance exists at the limit of the car's cornering power, then the car will tend to understeer at any lower cornering speed. If the vertical forces are symmetrical below the cornering limit, then over the range of speeds from that point up to the eventual limit the stagger torque will tend to cause oversteer. A "locked-and-staggered" car, in other words, has a path steer characteristic that is strongly dependent on cornering speed.

Predictably, the effects under braking are exactly the opposite—weight transfer from cornering still loads the right rear and unloads the left, but the direction of slip is reversed, so if the axle is braked while turning, the car will tend to turn toward whichever side is "heavier" at that particular cornering speed. As with acceleration, the extent of the effect is in proportion to the amount of slip.

We can't make too much of this, however, because the effect of the front brakes will further cloud the issue, but it seems safe to say that the weight transfer from cornering means that any longitudinal slip will create stagger torque, even if the amount of stagger is chosen to give theoretical free rolling at the given turn radius, at all but one cornering speed.

All other things equal, a vehicle with extreme left-side weight bias, like this supermodified, will be less prone to turn left with power on, and will show less variation in that tendency, than will a more symmetrical car. *Robin Hartford, Open Wheel Magazine*

There's another effect of stagger that we should mention. Running a smaller tire on one side will obviously tilt the entire axle down toward the smaller tire. That means that both tires will be running with a small—but significant—amount of camber. Some 9 1/2in of stagger (that's about 10 percent on a 30in tire) over a track width of 60in will produce nearly 1.5 degrees of camber. The lateral thrust from that camber will tend to shove the rear to the left when the car is running straight, and because that force is behind the mass center, it too will act to reduce the size of the stagger torque.

In fact, the whole issue is so complicated that about the only way to fix the ideal amount of stagger for any car on any track is by trial and error. Stagger is so tightly connected to so many other factors that affect handling that it's probably hopeless to try to arrive at any firm answers by a strict theoretical approach. Still, by breaking the picture down into parts, we hope that we may help to reduce the amount of guesswork—or at least chart some possible paths out of the woods—when changes produce unexpected results.

Though this sprinter, set up for a half-mile track, has only a modest amount of stagger, the cambering of both tires is clearly visible. This will both improve total cornering power and tend to reduce the left-turning tendency, because of the left-acting camber thrust. *Doug Gore, Open Wheel Magazine*

For a time, this gauge, made by StaggerMaster, was popular for measuring and comparing pairs of tires. A tape measure works well, too. *Jerry Haislip*

Chapter 9

Air is Free, Almost

If you've only remembered one thing so far, it should be this: the grip that a tire gets on pavement depends on the force pushing it onto the track. The amount of force it can develop—whether for acceleration, braking, or cornering—increases with every addition to this contact force. But though you can monkey around with the share of load carried by any one tire under any given set of circumstances by tinkering with the suspension, the *total* force on all four tires, no matter how it is distributed, always adds up to the same value—simply the weight of the car. What's needed is some way to press the tires harder onto the track, without adding weight in proportion. On pavement, at least, that's the whole point about wings.

How much extra contact force can a wing produce? A little calculation reveals that 24 square feet (sq-ft) of efficient wing running at 100mph can produce more than 1,800lb of force. If the wing is mounted right-side-up, as on an airplane, an 1,800lb car could *fly* at somewhere around 98mph! Of course, lifting all four wheels completely off the track is not the best arrangement for accelerating, steering, or stopping. But if the wing is turned upside-down, race car style, then it will roughly double the contact force sticking the car onto the track, meaning that braking distances will be potentially halved, acceleration doubled (assuming you have enough power to smoke the tires), and cornering speed increased by 40 percent. Eighteen hundred pounds of free traction!

Well, not quite. It takes power to shove that wing through the air. Even with a highly efficient wing shape and installation, the drag might still soak up more than 200hp at 100mph, and many of the wings on oval track race cars are much less efficient. That sounds like a big price to pay, but it is always worth spending a nickel to make a dime. When you have horsepower to spare, it is usually worth putting up with extra drag in exchange for more downforce. A convincing demonstration of this can be found in the practice times for Mike Mazur's supermodified in practice at Thompson International Speedway a few years ago. The car lost more than 10mph in maximum speed on the straights when its wing was mounted, but the extra traction permitted driver Bentley Warren to cut 1.5 seconds off the unwinged lap time.

The downforce
produced by a wing
depends on three things:
the size of the wing,
the speed,
and a number called
the *lift coefficient*.

The force the tires can exert to accelerate, stop, or turn a car depends on the force pressing them onto the ground. Wings increase that contact force, in some cases more than doubling it. Though a price is to be paid in drag, for high-powered cars, the additional force is almost always worth the cost. Why else would the cars with the big wings be leading the cars with the small wings? *Ken Simon*

The downforce produced by a wing depends on three things: the size of the wing, the speed, and a number called the *lift coefficient*. (Since wing technology and terminology come from airplanes, it is still called a lift coefficient, even though race cars run the wing inverted so the force acts downwards. The words *lift* and *downforce* are used interchangeably here.) For a wing of any given size running at a fixed speed, everything depends on the lift coefficient. The lift coefficient, in turn, is determined by the shape or profile of the wing and by how steeply it is angled into the air stream—a measurement called the *angle of attack*, or *angle of incidence*.

The relationship between downforce and incidence angle very much resembles the way the side force from a tire depends on how much the tire is steered. Each case involves a working range over

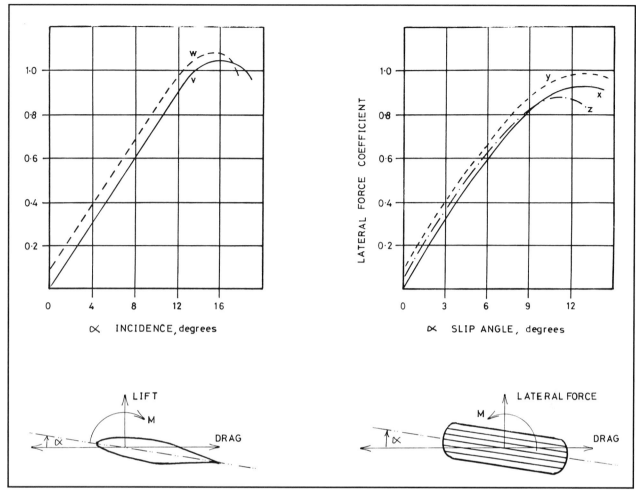

The ways wings and tires work are similar. Both generate a force at right angles to the way they're pointing when they are aimed at an angle to their direction of travel. Both develop a certain amount of drag as a price for the force they create. Both fade away as their working limit is reached.

which any small change in operating angle yields a proportional change in the force produced. But as some maximum value is approached, increases in the working angle have less and less effect, and at the bitter end, the force drops right off—more incidence gives less lift. The upper limit, which represents skidding in the case of tires, is called *stall* in the case of airfoils. A stalled wing produces very little lift, but lots of drag.

Like lift, the drag of a wing depends on speed, on the size of the wing, and on a number called the *drag coefficient*, which again is determined by the profile shape and the angle of attack. The drag actually has two components: *form drag* and *induced drag*. The first part is a property of the profile shape. Depending on the angle of attack, the difference between one airfoil profile and another can be quite large. Some airfoils are designed to operate most efficiently at small angles, others at large angles, in the same way that some engines are low-speed "torquers" and others have all their

For powerful cars on short tracks, it is usually worth trading drag for downforce. The problem boils down, then, to selecting a profile capable of the largest possible lift coefficient. Some shapes do better than others. Way better.

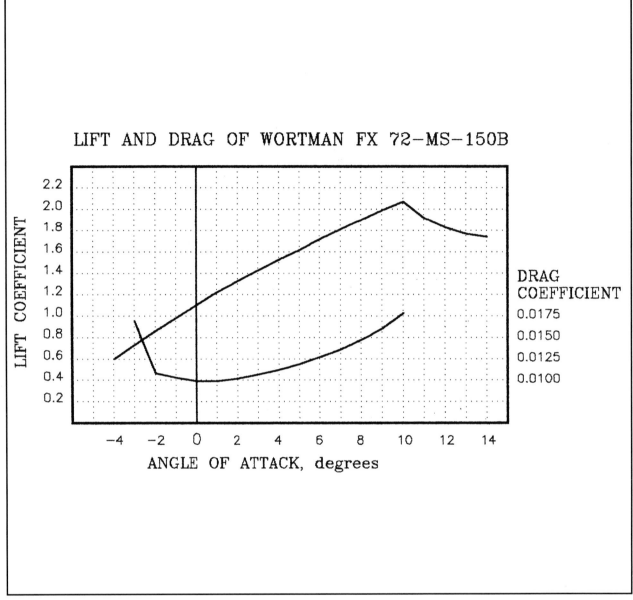

An efficient modern wing profile develops large amounts of
lift (upper curve, left-hand scale) for a relatively small
amount of drag (lower curve, right-hand scale).

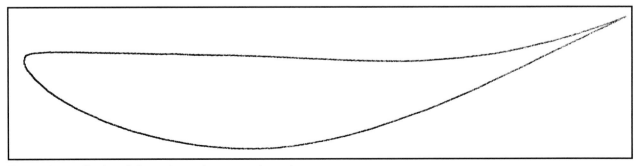

This is the profile that delivers the performance shown in
the previous graph—the Wortman FX 72-MS-150B.

Though they look small and primitive today, by the standards of 1973, when this photo was shot, these wings were pretty advanced. Some early wings were simply flat sheets of plywood. *Barrie Goodwin*

power at the top end. You can maximize the performance over one part of the range, but generally only at the expense of some other part.

The induced drag, on the other hand, is related to the lift developed. Think of it as the necessary price you pay for downforce, regardless of the shape of the profile. Because airplanes operate most of the time with very little lift in relation to the area of wing available, aircraft designers get high efficiency by selecting an airfoil that has the best ratio of lift to drag under cruise conditions. But race cars are limited by rules regulating how much wing area they can have, so they demand large amounts of downforce compared with the wing area. In these applications, variations in the form drag get swamped by the effect of the induced drag.

For example, one profile that has been used with success on various aircraft since the thirties, and by many early winged race cars, is called NACA 23012. (NACA stands for the National Advisory Committee for Aeronautics, the US agency that developed the NACA duct design.) At 7 degrees of incidence, it shows a lift coefficient of 0.85. A much more modern profile—Wortman FX 72-MS-150B—gives a lift coefficient of 1.81 at the same incidence. But if the Wortman wing is cranked back 9 degrees, it has the same lift coefficient as the NACA wing at 7 degrees, and so gives exactly the same downforce. If both wings measure 6ft by 4ft, at 100mph, both will produce a little less than 530lb of downforce; both will consume roughly 27hp. Surprisingly, at 100mph, even a flat sheet

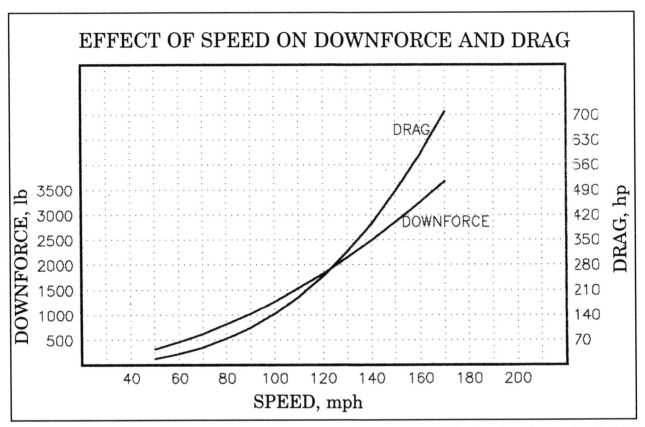

EFFECT OF SPEED ON DOWNFORCE AND DRAG

Both downforce and drag increase with speed, but if the drag is described in terms of the horsepower it soaks up, the drag rises faster. Compared with a reference speed of 100mph, by 150mph, the downforce is more than doubled and the drag is more than tripled.

Like lift, the drag of a wing depends on speed, on the size of the wing, and on a number called the *drag coefficient*, which again is determined by the profile shape and the angle of attack.

of plywood 6ft by 4ft with 9 degrees of incidence will produce... 522lb of downforce, for 27hp of drag!

Numbers like this have led one experienced aircraft designer to declare that it doesn't matter what kind of airfoil you use on a race car. What this individual has overlooked, though, is that racers are not usually looking for the best ratio of lift to drag. Let's say it again: For powerful cars on short tracks, it is usually worth trading drag for downforce. The problem boils down, then, to selecting a profile capable of the largest possible lift coefficient. Some shapes do better than others. Way better.

The flat sheet of plywood in the preceding example is already on the brink of stall at 9 degrees of incidence. The 522lb downforce at 100mph is all that is available—turning the angle up farther just increases the drag, while the downforce gets smaller. The NACA 23012, by comparison, can be cranked up to 14 degrees before it begins to "fall off the edge." At that angle, it will develop a healthy 922lb downforce at 100mph, in exchange for 76hp of drag. And the Wortman wing in this example is just loafing. At its peak of 10 degrees, it would soak up 144hp in drag, but it would produce a hefty 1,272lb downforce. So much for wings designed by "eyeball," and so much for certain experienced aircraft designers when it comes to race car wings!

If everything else is kept equal, both downforce and drag—expressed in pounds—vary with the square of the speed: double the speed yields four times the force. It is more usual and more useful, however, to express the drag of a wing in terms of horsepower. Since a pound of drag at

Because the optimum tradeoff between downforce and drag depends on the speed, some means of "trimming" the wing on the straights is desirable. On short tracks, the driver may be a bit too busy to cope with an extra control, though a left foot pedal might be manageable. Arranging for automatic adjustment would be ideal. *Doug Gore, Open Wheel Magazine*

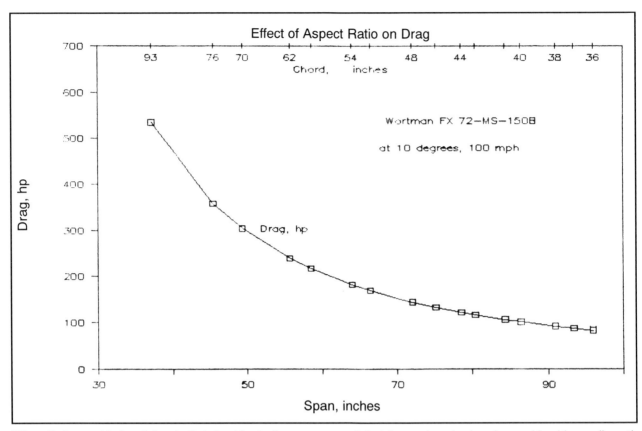

Effect of Aspect Ratio on Drag

Chord, inches

Wortman FX 72-MS-150B

at 10 degrees, 100 mph

Drag, hp

Drag, hp

Span, inches

Wings that are wide in relation to their front-back dimension are much more efficient than narrow ones with the same area. The downforce they create is not much different, but the savings in drag is considerable—well worth the trouble and expense of wasting some stock from a standard 6ft sheet of commercial aluminum.

100mph costs twice as much in horsepower as a pound of drag at 50mph, the drag in horsepower increases as the *cube* of the speed: doubling the speed costs eight times the drag in horsepower.

This rapid rise in lift and drag as speed increases presents racers with a real headache. Lots of grip is needed most for cornering, where race car speeds (and thus lift) are relatively low; on the straights, where speeds are higher, you're paying—with large amounts of drag—for downforce you don't need. When the wing is solidly mounted, the only solution is to establish the best compromise setting for each track: keep tipping the wing up until you start to go slower, then back off "a bit." Far better—if the rules allow it—is to arrange for the angle of incidence to be adjustable, either automatically or under the driver's control. The objective, for race cars as with aircraft, is obviously to get as much lift (downforce) as can be arranged when it is needed, for as little drag as possible.

Of course, if we could get the benefit of the downforce while reducing the drag, it would be better still. A variable that has a significant effect on the drag is the *aspect ratio*—the relation between the span and the front-to-back dimension, called the *chord*. (The aspect ratio influences lift

too, but much less than the drag.) For instance, our example assumes that the 24sq-ft of wing comes from a span of 72in and a chord of 48in. Many racers use wings 6ft wide because that is the size of standard sheets of aluminum. If we increase the span to 80in and reduce the chord to 43.2in to keep the area at 24sq-ft, the 144hp drag of the Wortman wing will be reduced to 117hp for the same 1,272lb downforce at 100mph.

Another factor that affects drag is whether endplates are fitted, and their height. The purpose of endplates is to prevent air "spilling over" from the high-pressure surface of the wing—the top, in our case—to the low-pressure side. This leakage wastes some of the work done by the wing and shows up as increased drag. If the 80in-by-43.2in Wortman wing in our example had endplates 1ft high, the drag would drop still further to 102hp. Using endplates 2ft high would cut it down to 83hp. Fortunately, the practical limit for endplate height roughly corresponds to the point where the law of diminishing returns starts to set in.

Whether you are shopping for a ready-made wing or planning to make your own, the first thing to do in choosing a suitable profile is to lay your hands on a collection of graphs—called *polars*—of

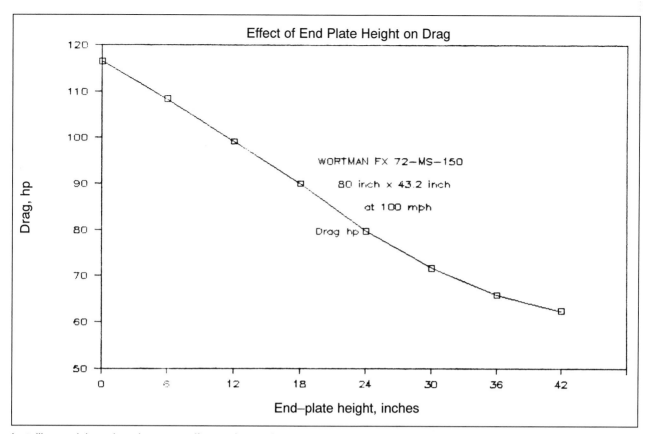

Effect of End Plate Height on Drag

WORTMAN FX 72-MS-150

80 inch x 43.2 inch

at 100 mph

Drag hp

Installing endplates has the same effect as increasing the ratio of the span to the chord. Fortunately, most of the benefit can be achieved with endplates of practical size.

different airfoil characteristics. The graph labeled "Lift and Drag of Wortman FX 72-MS-150B" is an example. Thousands of these have been painstakingly constructed from wind tunnel work around the world over the years. One excellent source is *Theory of Wing Sections* by Ira Abbott and Albert von Doenhoff, published in paperback by Dover Publications. The library at any university with an engineering school should have, in addition, similar information on more modern and more specialized airfoils. Information on the Wortman airfoil, for instance, is given in *A Catalog of Low Reynolds Number Airfoil Data for Wind Turbine Applications* compiled by S. J. Miley of Texas A & M University. All you have to do is ask the reference librarian, and take along a bag of dimes for the photocopy machine. It's easy! Along with the polars you will find tables of coordinates that give the positions of points on the top and bottom surfaces of the airfoil, expressed as a percentage of the chord length, so you can draw the wing profile, marked out in full scale on aluminum if you like.

Once you've built or bought a wing, the next thing to attend to is mounting it. When you consider that the loads on the wing can equal or exceed the weight of the car, the mountings need to be

hefty indeed. There's no point in building a miniature Brooklyn Bridge on top of the car, though, because if the wing mounts clutter up the airflow, you won't be getting much downforce anyway. A well-designed race car wing can outperform a sheet of plywood because it manages to bend the air upwards without the airflow separating from its surface. This is no problem on the high-pressure (top) side, but air is a lot easier to push than to pull, so the air on the low-pressure underside is just looking for some excuse to break away. To function effectively, the wing needs a clean flow of air on both top and bottom surfaces. It should be kept as far as possible away from any bodywork or structure, and the mounts should be well streamlined and faired smoothly into the wing surface.

One solution that has been used by Indy and Formula One cars is to mount the wing from the endplates only. Beware, however, of the large bending loads in the wing itself. Though small race car wings can get away with just a sheet of aluminum wrapped around flanged ribs cut to the right profile, mounting from the endplates pretty much demands a structural spar running spanwise inside the wing. Also, if you elect to use a wing that adjusts its own angle of attack, the wing

Whatever holds the wing up had better be sturdy—the forces are large, and get larger real fast with increasing speed. George Marshall (right) encountered this problem in his first outing on a mile track. *Jack Gladback*

On the other hand, the wing mountings tend to clutter up the airflow. Though this builder has provision for adjustment in every conceivable direction, including sideways, the airflow under the wing will be seriously disturbed by all that hardware. *Robin Hartford, Open Wheel Magazine*

Indy cars used to maintain clean flow to the bottom surface of the wing by mounting the airfoil by its endplates. Nowadays, this sort of pylon mounting is universal. In ei-ther case, the wing itself has to be structurally rugged to withstand the bending loads. *Doug Gore, Open Wheel Magazine*

might oscillate between up and down at some critical speed. To avoid this, you will either have to use a damper of some kind or else arrange for some sort of toggle action so that the wing latches up at a lower speed than it latches down.

Gusts of wind, turbulence from other cars, or movement of the car on its suspension can change the effective angle of attack, so it is important to ensure that the wing starts off well short of its stalling angle. With the front suspension bottomed-out and the rear suspension at its upward limit of travel, the wing should still be at least 1 or 2 degrees on the safe side of its maximum incidence angle.

A handful of designs do even better than the Wortman airfoil we've been discussing, but the search for more downforce from a limited wing size usually leads to slotted flaps. Some race rules prohibit multi-element wings, but if the ones you are following permit them, slotted flaps are definitely worth exploring. Though the "flying car" example at the beginning of this chapter is actually based on a wing with a slotted flap, we haven't touched on this subject here because it is just too tough to give useful examples. The performance of a wing with a slotted flap depends on the profile of the wing itself, the profile of the flap, the size and angle of attack of the flap in relation to the wing, the shape of the lip at the trailing edge of the wing, the size of the slot, and a few other things. It gets even worse in the case of double slotted flaps. You'll find information on slotted flaps in *Theory of Wing Sections*.

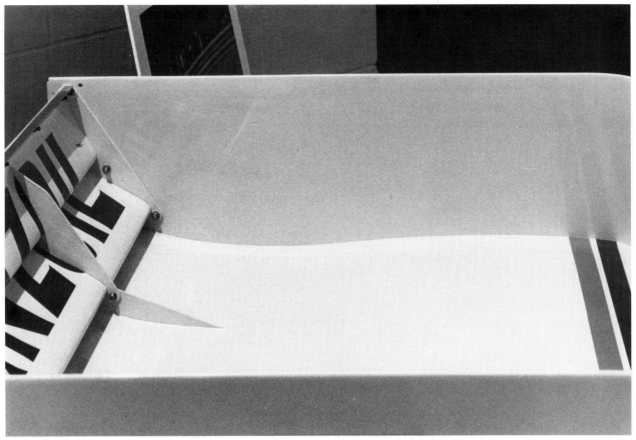

Double slotted flaps work even better, in terms of maximum downforce. Where permitted, such "cascade" airfoils outperform any single-element wing. *Doug Gore, Open Wheel Magazine*

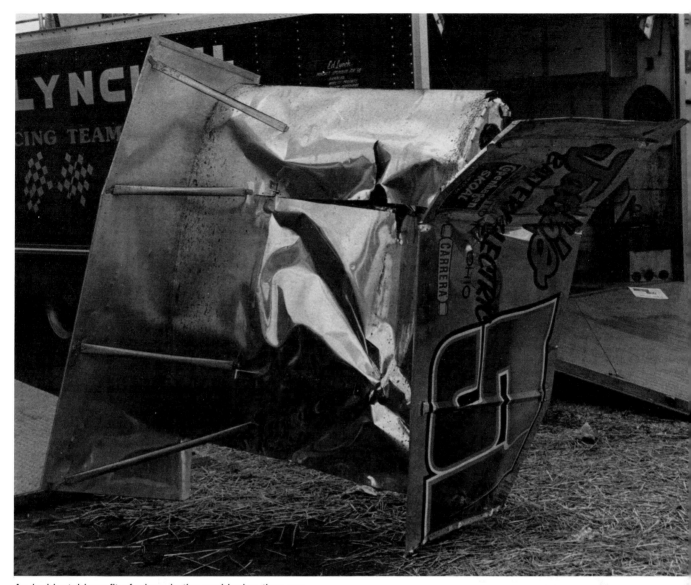

An incidental benefit of wings is the cushioning they provide when the car flips. It tends to be rough on the wings, though. *Doug Gore, Open Wheel Magazine*

Left
A slotted flap bends the air farther than is possible with any single airfoil section. The slot permits a controlled amount of high-pressure air to leak through to the low-pressure side of the flap, postponing the tendency for the airflow to separate when it is bent too far. The gain from the added curvature of the air stream more than makes up for the loss from the "leak." *Doug Gore, Open Wheel Magazine*

Chapter 10

The Air Above, The Mud Below

Now it's time to consider the rather special situation of wings on dirt, so start working on your pilot's license!

A wing works very differently on a dirt car than it does on a pavement racer. Under some conditions, a dirt car wing may be little more than a convenient mounting bracket for the endplates.

Cars have been racing on dirt for quite a while longer than they have been racing on pavement. Despite that, very little published information is available about factors that affect the handling of race cars on dirt. This contrasts strongly with the mountain of information about their behavior on pavement. In view of this near-universal ignorance, we might approach the subject of dirt car wings with considerable hesitation—though an advantage of talking about a subject so little understood is that it is hard for anyone to prove you wrong!

First, the interlocking between dirt tires and the track surface results in a "rack-and-pinion" effect. In fact, both dirt and pavement tires mechanically mesh with the surface. On dirt, the tire indents the track to some extent, depending on how soft the track is. On pavement, the tire rubber actually flows around the rough texture of the track surface—it is the track that indents the tire. Asphalt is stronger than rubber, so when a tire "slips" on pavement, part of the rubber gets torn off—that's what the black marks are made of. In loose dirt, a tire does not slip in the same way; rather, it tears away part of the track surface, because rubber is stronger than dirt. This puts dirt cars at a disadvantage, in terms of pure side bite.

In terms of forward bite, however, this "cogwheel" effect means that the amount of traction force available on a loose surface depends partly on the amount of dirt sheared off and pumped rearward by the tires. Unlike tires on pavement, which give less forward thrust when they slip more than a few percent, tires on dirt may actually give more traction in the forward direction with wheel spin. Of course, forwards and sideways are not easily defined with a dirt car. And when forward becomes sideways, the thrust of this "dirt pump" is directed toward the center of the turn. This likely provides a substantial share of the force that pushes a dirt car around a corner. But what does all this have to do with wings?

On pavement, the whole point of wings is to press the tires harder onto the track. Every addition to the force of contact with the ground increases the amount of traction force the tire can deliver—whether for acceleration, braking, or cornering.

Part of the force that propels a race car on dirt comes from the same frictional interaction with the surface that tires develop on pavement. Another part comes from shearing off pieces of track—pumping mud, in other words. The photographer reports that "yes, those wet clumps do hurt!" *Dave Olson*

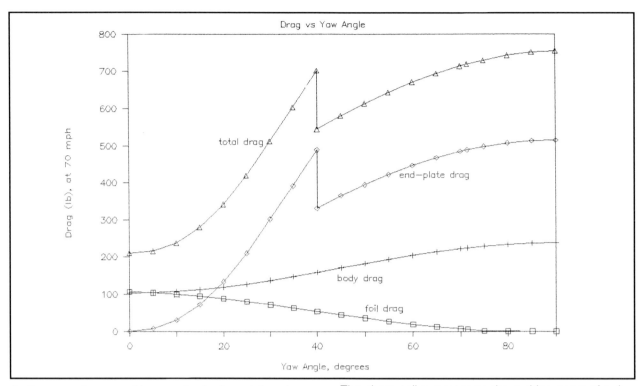

As the car gets more sideways, the body and the wing endplates turn to face the breeze, creating a sizable drag force that slows the car. Meanwhile, the wing itself, partly in the shadow of the upstream endplate, creates less drag.

The sharp spike represents the sudden onset of turbulence that occurs when air flows over a flat plate at the critical angle of about 40 degrees.

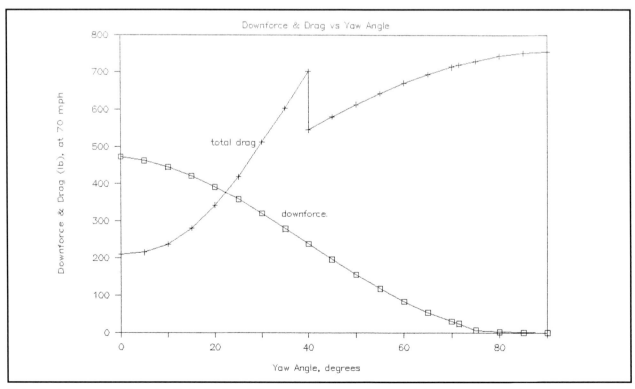

Not only does more of the wing lie in the lee of the endplate as the yaw angle increases, also the air is flowing over the rest of the wing at an angle, so it develops less downforce. The drag just keeps on climbing, though.

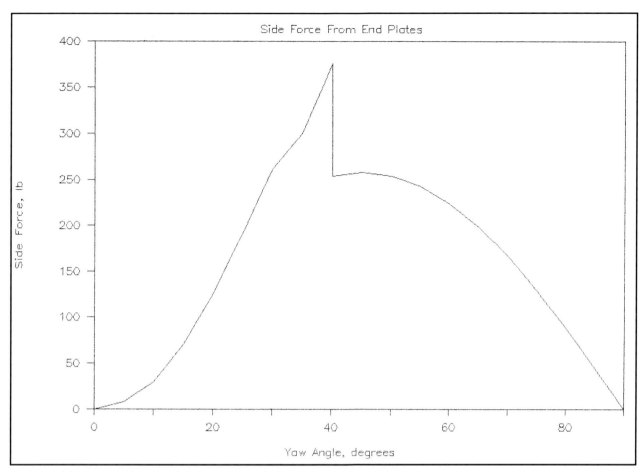

As forward becomes sideways, drag becomes side force. At the peak of the curve, the component of the force acting toward the center of the turn can become sizable.

On pavement, the whole point of wings is to press the tires harder onto the track. Every addition to the force of contact with the ground increases the amount of traction force the tire can deliver—whether for acceleration, braking, or cornering. Though this effect is doubtless part of the explanation of what wings do for dirt cars, their main influence in this case may lie in other areas. Because dirt cars get so far sideways, the air is often not flowing over the wing from front to back. At worst, the wing is working entirely sideways, along with the rest of the car. Now, air is air, no matter what kind of ground surface is under it, and a wing simply cannot produce any useful downforce when the air is flowing over it sideways. What is more, by the time the car gets pointed sufficiently straight down the track for the wing to add significant downforce, a big wing may be costing more in drag than the increased traction is worth. Yet wings make dirt cars faster.

Usually, wings make race cars faster because they help cornering more than they hurt speed on the straights. But here, we have a situation where the wing must be hurting on the straights, yet—in extreme cases—it can't possibly produce much downforce in the corners. Okay, if a dirt car will go faster with a wing than without one, but the wing isn't making the difference, what is? One explanation may be the huge endplates used on dirt car wings. It seems likely these endplates are as important as the wing itself. Maybe more so.

Consider an arrangement consisting of a 24sq-ft wing with endplates measuring 3ft by 6ft. In a typical setup, the endplates are vertically staggered, with the left-side plate mostly above the wing and the right one mostly below it. As seen from the side, the total area of endplates could amount to as much as 36sq-ft—50 percent more area than that of the wing itself. Assuming a wing of average efficiency, the downforce at, say, 70mph will amount to about 470lb, and will cost about 120lb in drag. That's when the car is pointed straight ahead.

When the car gets sideways, however, it moves at an angle to the air stream, and the picture changes. First, part of the wing will be in the

The aerodynamic force from the endplates is great enough to rip out three rivets, and its loss definitely slowed driver Tom Bigelow in the turns when his endplate failed. *Jack Gladback*

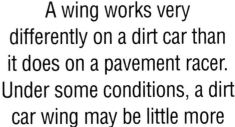

"shadow" of the upstream endplate, so only part of its area will be functional. Second, the area that *is* working will have the air flowing over it at an angle, so its downforce—and drag, for that matter—will be reduced. Finally, as the side area of the car and the wing endplates turn to face the breeze, their combined area will also develop a substantial amount of drag. Without data from actual tests, we can only estimate these effects, so all the accompanying graphs are approximations arrived at after talking to some people in the aircraft business. (The aircraft folks also supplied the term *yaw angle*—the angle between the way the car is pointing and the way it is actually going.)

These graphs show that if we turn the car completely sideways, so the wing is moving endplate-on to the air, the downforce drops to near zero. At the same time, the drag—against the direction the car is moving—amounts to 755lb at the same 70mph. We estimate 515lb comes from the

A wing works very differently on a dirt car than it does on a pavement racer. Under some conditions, a dirt car wing may be little more than a convenient mounting bracket for the endplates.

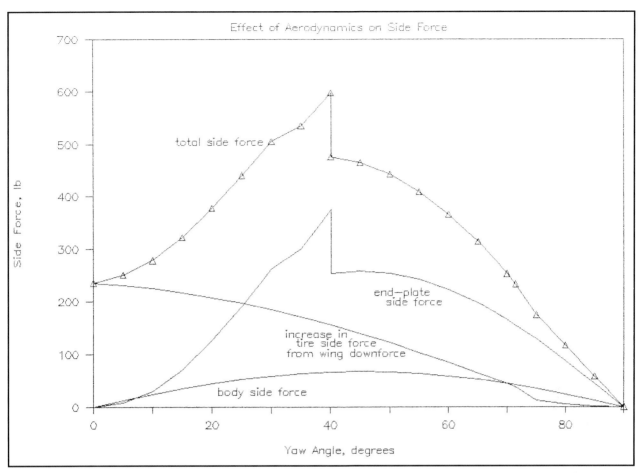

The downforce from a wing increases the cornering force provided by the tires, but the wing becomes progressively less effective as it is turned side-on to the breeze. At the same time, the endplates—and, to a lesser extent, the car body—produce a force that first rises, then falls, as the yaw angle increases. The curve for total side force makes clear that the endplates play a major role.

endplates; the remaining 240lb comes from 26sq-ft of bodyside area. Of course, a force acting against the direction the car is going does nothing except slow the car down; that's part of the reason totally sideways is not the fastest way around.

The interesting thing is that at smaller yaw angles, part of the wind force against the body side and wing endplates is still creating drag—though less of it—but another part of the same force acts toward the center of the turn. The body and endplates are effectively acting as rudders, helping to shove the car around the turn. The adjacent graph shows a best guess about the size of the side force from the endplates.

The sharp spike that first catches your eye in the accompanying diagram—and in all the other curves that relate to endplate forces—is no mistake. It reflects the sudden transition from the endplate behaving as an airfoil—causing the air to divide cleanly and flow over both sides—to its behaving as a bluff body. (*Bluff body* is an aerodynamic term meaning any unstreamlined, solid

lump.) At small yaw angles, the airflow is able to change direction smoothly around the surfaces of the endplate, and the side force from the plates rises fairly steadily to a peak of about 375lb. But a critical point is reached at about 40 degrees when the airflow can no longer stay attached to the "downstream" face of the plate.

At that point, the flow breaks away and becomes turbulent. The oncoming air is still impacting the "upstream" side of the plate, but the benefit of a strong suction on the downstream face has been lost, and the side force drops very suddenly by about a third, to about 250lb. From there on, it fades steadily away until, by 90 degrees, nothing is left. Remember that even though the force of the air against the endplate is very large at this point, the car is turned completely sideways, so the force is acting directly against the car's forward motion—none of it is aimed toward the center of the turn.

On a car weighing, say, 1,700lb including driver and fuel, the 375lb of endplate side force in this example would produce up to 0.22G of corner-

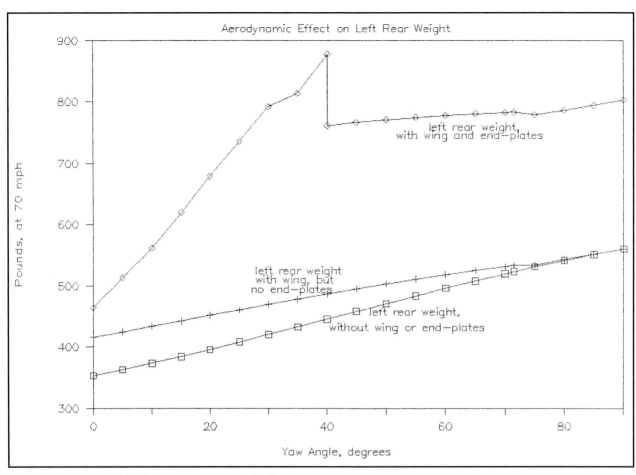

<figure>
Aerodynamic Effect on Left Rear Weight

left rear weight, with wing and end-plates

left rear weight with wing, but no end-plates

left rear weight, without wing or end-plates

Pounds, at 70 mph

Yaw Angle, degrees
</figure>

Not only do the endplate forces shove the car bodily toward the center of the turn, they also roll it inboard, increasing the load on the left rear tire.

ing force all by itself, without the tires doing anything. On a loose surface, this 0.22G could amount to about half of the total cornering power. It is useful to describe the grip of a tire-surface combination in terms of the force of gravity. Without a wing, race tires on pavement can develop a side force equal to 1.2-1.5 times the weight of the car, so with maximum driver effort, the car could corner at 1.2G to 1.5G. Wings clamp the tires harder onto the track, increasing the maximum cornering power, so Indy cars can reach 2.5G or more. On a dirt surface, the basic grip may range from a low of 0.2G or 0.3G, to a high of 0.7G or 0.8G.

Another interesting aspect of this is that the side force from the endplates increases with increasing yaw, while the downforce of the wing itself—and so its ability to improve side bite—is fading. The tradeoff between these two effects is plotted in the "Effect of Aerodynamics on Side Force" diagram in this chapter. The bottom curve shows the minor effect of the bodyside area. The next curve up indicates the contribution the wing's downforce makes to cornering. It shows the in-

crease in cornering power provided by the wing, on a surface that could provide 0.5G of cornering power without a wing. The next-higher curve shows the cornering force produced directly by the endplates; this is the same curve as shown in the previous figure. The total of these three aerodynamic effects is shown in the top curve.

Again, some hedging is in order: all these curves are based on calculations, and the calculations themselves are based on estimated values. In other words, though better than pure guesswork, these numbers are not guaranteed! Still, as long as the logic is sound, a couple of things seem clear even if the numbers are off by a lot. First, at large yaw angles, the endplates account for more side force than the wing does. Second, the peak occurs at somewhere around 40 degrees of yaw—that particular number is most likely accurate—and things get worse from there on. Finally, the side force from the endplates acting as rudders may match and—on large, fast tracks or on very loose surfaces—even exceed the side force from the tires.

Note also that the endplate forces are acting 5ft

Any doubt about the size of the aerodynamic forces that endplates deliver should be erased by, first, the impressive inward roll angle of Jack Haudenschild's sprinter and, second, the deformation apparent in the right-side endplate. *Gordon Gill*

or more above the ground. One result of this is the familiar inward tilt of a dirt car—the impact of the air on the high-mounted endplates is overwhelming the natural tendency of the car to roll to the outside. Examining photos with a protractor suggests that this *negative roll* can reach 15 degrees.

An incidental effect of this is that the wing's downforce no longer acts straight down; part of it is now directed toward the right side of the car. Unless the car is completely sideways, this "adverse side force" is aimed partly toward the *outside* of the turn, fighting the efforts of the endplates and tires! The negative roll reaches large values, however, only at large yaw angles, and by then, the wing is skewed around so far that this adverse side force points more forwards than sideways—remember, it isn't easy to distinguish between the two! Also, the wing's downforce is pretty well washed out by that point, from operating sideways, so overall, this ef-

fect is probably not significant.

One result of this negative rolling force that *does* seem to be significant is the effect it has on tire loading. We have tried to show how the left rear weight varies according to yaw angle in the accompanying diagram, labeled "Aerodynamic Effect on Left Rear Weight." The bottom curve is for a car with no wing or endplates; the middle curve takes account of the downforce from a wing but assumes no side force from endplates; the top curve shows the result of adding in the endplate side force.

It may at first seem confusing that the load on the left rear tire increases as the car gets more sideways, even when no aerodynamic effects are figured in. Remember, though, that if the car is traveling in an arc, with its nose pointed right at the center of the arc, the load transfer is no longer toward the right side of the *car*, but rather to the right side of the *turn*—which means toward the *rear* of the car... which hammers home the message that race car dynamics is a tricky business.

With a locked rear end, increasing the load on the left rear has two effects. First, it directly improves the car's traction. Second, because the left rear can now push forward harder, it tends to make the car turn *clockwise* around its own center of gravity. The increase in understeer, or push, may not seem desirable, but it can have a remarkable effect on stability if it occurs just as the car tries to get out of shape sideways.

Imagine our hypothetical race car running well balanced through a turn at 70mph, at anything up to, say, a 30-degree yaw angle. Now look at what happens if for any reason it starts getting loose: as it begins to yaw farther in the counterclockwise direction, the wind force on the endplates increases, levering weight onto the left rear tire. The additional forward thrust from the left rear tries to rotate the car clockwise, so the two effects tend to cancel each other out. Even if the cancellation isn't complete, the result is still a useful contribution to stability, making the car more controllable.

Accepting that our analysis here is fairly valid, we can draw some lessons from all of this. First, it appears that the wing itself has less to do with the performance of a dirt car than do the endplates it holds up. Second, the endplates may account for a significant fraction of the total cornering power of a winged dirt car; on some surfaces at some speeds, they may be the largest single contributor to cornering power, more important even than the tires. Finally, the ability of the endplates to increase left rear tire load with increases in yaw angle adds a significant amount of stability to the behavior of the car, at least up to 40 degrees of yaw.

The large yaw angles exhibited by dirt race cars create some complex interactions, and this maze of interrelationships forces a realization that the whole business is much more complicated than the situation on pavement, where you can assume that the car generally goes the way it is pointed, give or take a few degrees.

Winged cars aren't the only ones that can benefit from the rudder effect. This outlaw mini is on the right track, though the struts would have an easier time of it if this huge vertical plate were on the other side of the car. *Bob Fairman*

Chapter 11

The Fifth Spring

Torsional stiffness is not the only criterion for a chassis frame, but it is an important one. Here's why stiffness is significant, and how to get it.

Here's a mystery for you: Some oval track racers—winners included—claim that a bit of flex in the frame doesn't hurt; they say in fact, it helps the car conform to the track... or words to that effect. Yet Indy and Formula One teams are spending upwards of $50,000 apiece to get a frame so stiff that if you embedded one end in a concrete wall and parked a Buick on the end of a 6ft Johnson bar attached to the other end, you couldn't tweak it out of square by 1 degree. What's going on here?

One clue is the acknowledgment by the flexy fliers that a stiff frame *may* be better, *if* the suspension setup is right on the money. Flex in the chassis, they say, offers a lot of latitude in chassis settings; a stiff car is more difficult to set up correctly.

To understand what may be happening, we have to back up a bit. Recall that for typical beam axle race cars on pavement, the basic handling characteristics are largely a matter of how the forces that resist roll get divided up between the two ends of the car. As the car tries to roll in corners, the springs and A/R bars fight back. As a result, the load transfer from the inside tire to the outside at each end of the car depends on the stiffness of the springs and A/R bars at each end. The end with more roll stiffness will see more load change and so will wipe out first.

But this only works if the frame stays put. If the frame is springy, the stiff end sheds part of its load by winding up the frame, which tends to equalize the roll stiffness between ends. A car with a wiggly frame, then, responds less to changes in spring and roll bar rates than a car with a stiff frame. Since juggling the front-rear distribution of roll stiffness is one of the basic ways of tuning the handling of a race car, using a flexible frame makes the setup harder to get wrong but impossible to get right. This is likely the resolution of the mystery of the stiff frame.

> In a stiff frame, strength is not usually an issue, except incrashes. A well-made frame that has enough stiffness will more or less automatically be strong enough to carry all the working loads with lots of might to spare.

It can be useful to think of the frame as a giant torsion bar connecting the suspension at the two ends of the car—a "fifth spring." If the car works well with roughly equal roll stiffness at each end, then it really doesn't matter how stiff that torsion bar is... as long as the track is perfectly flat, or until you have to make a transition from turning to going straight, or vice versa. Then you would notice that any time the loading changes, the fifth spring oscillates back and forth; no damping occurs—this spring has no shock absorber! For beam axle cars, this is one objection to a limber frame.

Another problem: in reality, most race cars don't handle best with equal roll stiffness at both ends. If the torsional stiffness of the frame is low in relation to the difference in roll stiffness between the two ends, the car will be insensitive to changes in springs and A/R bars.

Also, all our discussion so far is based on the assumption that we're dealing with a beam axle car, where camber is set by the axle beam. Independent suspension—at either end—absolutely demands a stiff frame; otherwise, the tire camber angles keep changing as the frame warps around. One rule of thumb for race cars with independent suspension is that the torsional stiffness of the frame should be at least ten times the difference in roll stiffness between front and rear suspensions, to prevent interactions of this kind. It would be interesting to know how many experiments with independent suspension on oval track cars were abandoned simply because the frame wasn't stiff enough.

In a stiff frame, strength is not usually an issue, except in crashes. A well-made frame that has enough stiffness will more or less automatically be strong enough to carry all the working loads with lots of might to spare. In fact, the extra structural

The most efficient way to carry a torsional load is with a big tube, the bigger the better. This Indy car's circular shape is not just for slick appearance—the working loads are carried by the skin surface, and the skin is as "big" as you can get without making the car larger. *Larry Van Sickle*

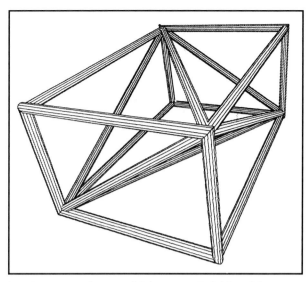

In a true space frame, all tubes are straight and there are no unsupported rectangular spaces. Each welded joint could be replaced by a hinge without affecting stiffness. Though it makes for tricky—and sometimes impractical—welding, next to monocoque construction, this arrangement gives the most stiffness for a given weight.

beef needed to cope with the "contact sport" nature of open-wheel racing means surplus material is available to take care of stiffness—leaving few excuses for a wobbly frame. A frame that isn't well made, however—one with funky welds, for instance—can show decent stiffness, yet break in normal racing use.

Second, we're talking about *torsional* stiffness here—the spring rate of that giant fifth-spring torsion bar. A frame with sufficient stiffness in torsion will almost always have a surplus of stiffness against simple "beaming"—the bending force that tends to make the car sag in the middle.

The usual way of gauging frame stiffness is not far from our Buick–on–a–Johnson bar method: you anchor one end of the chassis frame to something solid, then fasten a beam across the other end and, using the beam as a lever, try to twist the frame. By measuring the amount of torque it takes to wind up the frame by 1 degree, you get a figure for chassis stiffness. Race car frames run all the way from a couple of hundred pounds-feet (lb-ft) of torque per degree of twist, to over 10,000lb-ft per degree… way over, in some cases: a torque of 6

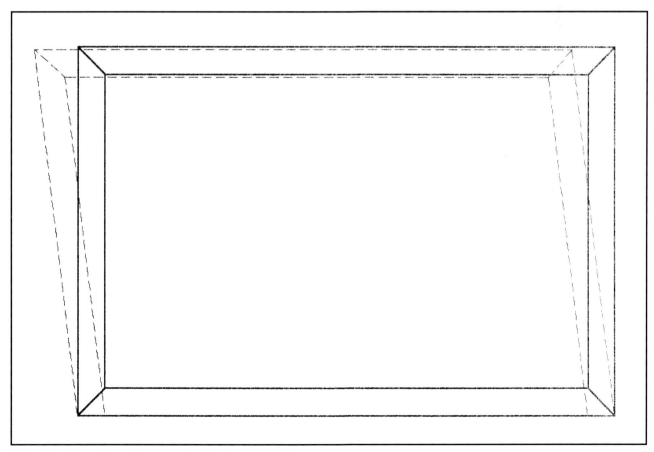

Without a diagonal member, a rectangle of welded tubing depends on the stiffness of the corner joints to prevent distortion into a diamond or lozenge shape.

Though doubtless strong enough, this sprint car frame is not an efficient structure. Loads that tend to distort the frame end up trying to bend tubes. The idea is to arrange for those loads to try to stretch or compress tubes. *Jack Gladback*

Providing a rigid connection between the front and rear suspensions is one vital task for the frame, but it is not the only one; the frame also has to hold the engine, the driver, and the fuel in place.

Buicks-feet per degree of twist would not be much of an exaggeration for a modern Indy chassis. The accompanying table summarizes the measured torsional stiffness and weight of a wide variety of race cars.

It's easy to make a stiff frame: a giant slab of concrete will do fine. Getting decent stiffness for a reasonable weight is tougher. Note from the table that the 1968 STP Indy turbine car, *Silent Sam*, showed over 30,000lb-ft per degree, yet the structure weighed just 137lb. Indy "roadsters" of just a few years earlier had frames that weighed about the same, but had at most one-thirtieth the torsional stiffness. Current Indy cars are claiming 25,000lb-ft per degree to 30,000lb-ft per degree from a structure weighing about 70lb to 90lb.

From a stiffness-to-weight point of view, the most efficient torsion bar is a big tube—preferably

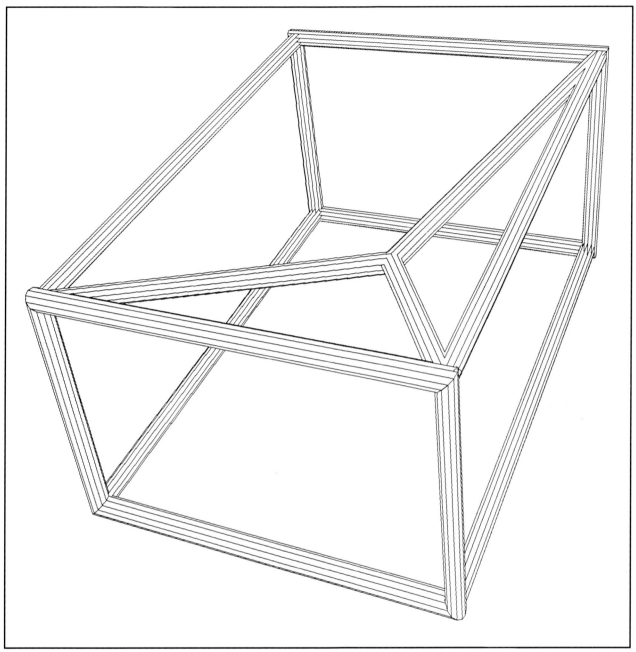

A diagonal can be offset around obstructions without reducing stiffness or increasing weight by much. The same technique can be used to stiffen the shared bulkheads between subsections of a space frame.

round, and the bigger the better. A big square or rectangular tube is next best, and is a more practical shape. That is basically what every Indy and Formula One monocoque amounts to, at least from the roll bar forwards.

A problem with a single giant tube, though, is providing access to all the machinery. Also, a large fabricated tube is difficult to fix, and expensive to replace. With mid-engined cars, the works are all out back, behind the monocoque center section, and—in Indy and Formula One, at least—a sponsor with very deep pockets usually covers the tab

for the tub when things get crumpled. For front-engined cars, a conventional tube frame is not just the only way to ensure access to all the hot and noisy parts, it is likely all a private owner can afford—especially if it is likely to get bent.

From the table, it looks as if tube frames can't come anywhere close to the performance of a monocoque, but the situation may not be as bad as it seems. For starters, the tube frames showing the poorest numbers are not really space frames. A *space frame* isn't just a bunch of tubes welded into a box shape, it is a very specific form of construc-

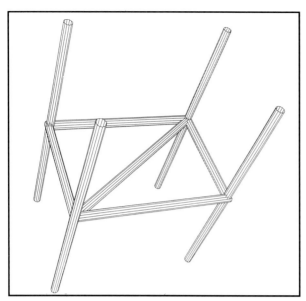

Where a large unobstructed hole through the middle of a bulkhead is needed, a double-hoop stiffener may be used, supported by a lattice of lighter tubing.

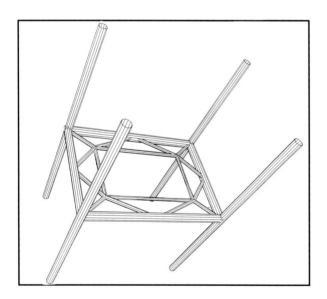

and strong—structure. Perhaps less widely appreciated is the fact that, to be of maximum benefit, *each* rectangular face must be triangulated. Diagonals across five of the six faces of the rectangle are better than none, but it's like a chain with one rubber link: serious stiffness isn't achieved until the structure is complete. One diagonal is sufficient; anyplace you have a pair of them forming an *X*, one of the diagonals is redundant.

Providing a rigid connection between the front

It's easy to make a stiff frame: a giant slab of concrete will do fine. Getting decent stiffness for a reasonable weight is tougher.

and rear suspensions is one vital task for the frame, but it is not the only one; the frame also has to hold the engine, the driver, and the fuel in place. For these and other practical reasons, space frames are usually arranged as two or three smaller boxes, joined together end to end. Each of these "bays" must be a complete, fully triangulated structure itself, though it is okay for two adjacent bays to share one panel.

It is normally a simple matter to triangulate the sides of each bay. Fitting stiffening diagonals into the top and bottom surfaces is often trickier. How will you get the engine in or out, for instance? One way is to make the diagonal removable. From an engineering point of view, this is perfectly acceptable, but care has to be taken in the design of the bolted joints. A different method of dodging around an obstruction is to use a Y-shaped diagonal.

Of course, you can duck the problem of fitting a tube frame around the engine by using the engine itself as a structural member. This is common practice; the only points of concern are to ensure that you don't overload thin engine castings, particularly if they are aluminum, and to avoid using both the engine *and* a tubular framework to span the same gap. Iron expands when hot, aluminum grows even more, and there is a real risk of either ripping the tubework apart or warping the motor as the engine warms up. Thought should also be given to the effect of vibration on the framework and its welds.

tion in which every tube is straight and is loaded in pure tension or compression. In a proper space frame, every welded joint could be replaced with a ball joint without affecting stiffness. That is a good deal easier to say than to do; at the very least, it requires some labor-intensive fitting and some very fancy welding.

The lightest, simplest, and least expensive space frame would consist of a large rectangular box with a diagonal across each face. The point of the diagonal tubes is to prevent the rectangles they span from distorting into a diamond shape under load. Most racers recognize the triangles created by these diagonals as the key to a stiff—

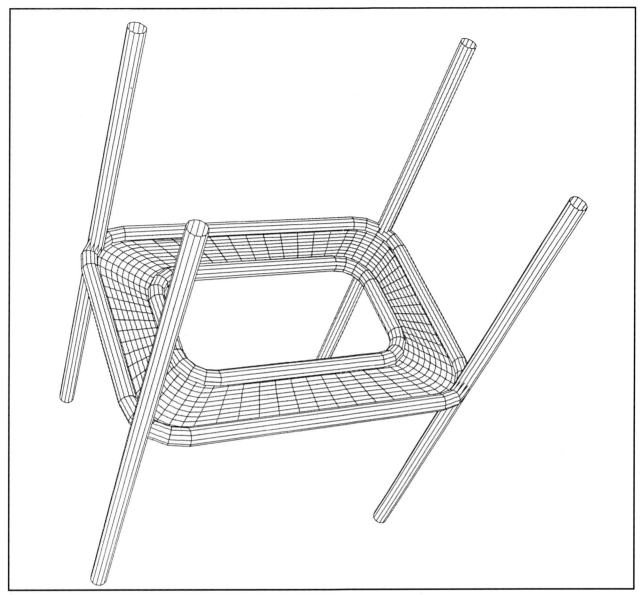

As an alternative to the complicated latticework seen previously, you can also stiffen a double-hoop bulkhead by paneling the space between the hoops with sheet metal. You can even drill the sheet metal full of holes, if you like, to save weight.

The bulkheads that join the bays are another problem area: the driver's legs and the drive shaft often poke through one of these. Though a split diagonal might be possible, an alternative is a double "hoop," either lattice braced or skinned over with sheet metal, as suggested in the illustrations. This kind of construction has been used in aircraft since they were first made of metal. Though heavier than a simple diagonal, the double hoop stiffens the bulkhead while leaving a large useful space through the middle. The same technique can be used to stiffen the cockpit opening, though a roll cage—fully triangulated and integrated into the rest of the chassis—can likely do a better job.

High rigidity in some localized areas of the frame does not help overall stiffness much—though it does create very high local stresses. On the other hand, seemingly small areas of local springiness can seriously impair an otherwise satisfactory design. For instance, "downtube"-type frames for sprint cars are sometimes believed to have increased torsional stiffness. In truth, though beaming stiffness is likely increased a good bit, the gain in torsion is not great, unless unusual attention is paid to the bulkheads that join the two sides.

The objective is to get the maximum spring rate out of the structure that joins the front suspension to the back, so the spring loads have to be fed

OK, so there's lots of triangles. But they almost all lie in the planes of the sides of the frame. This kind of structure is great for resisting beaming loads—the kind that make the frame sag in the middle—but the lack of triangulation when viewed from above or from the ends compromises torsional stiffness. *Doug Gore, Open Wheel Magazine*

into the corners of the space frame. It does no good at all to build a killer stiff frame, then to connect the springs to the main structure through springy, overhung brackets or to mount the springs near the middle of an unsupported span of tubing.

True space frames have some problems. First, practical considerations make it almost impossible to create a geometrically correct structure—you can't very well run a diagonal across the windshield area, for instance. Also, to be geometrically correct, you wind up with an awful lot of tubes coming together at single joints. Though this works OK with very lightweight tubing, as used on aircraft and lightweight road race cars, the thicker-walled tubing typical of oval track racers is prone to weld failures if the same technique is employed.

Still, the principles remain valid, even if in many places pure space frame principles have to be sacrificed to practical considerations. Though some racers in every era have triumphed despite willowy frames, it is difficult to argue that they have won because of them.

Remember, whether you are planning to roll your own chassis or just figuring to add a subframe for some purpose to an existing chassis, a well-engineered frame is always designed last—though it may be the first part built, to provide a convenient assembly platform. The right approach is to first figure out where the parts have to go, then design the frame so that it connects all their mounting points together.

Stiffness and Weight—Various Chassis

Vehicle	Frame Type	Material	Torsional Stiffness lb-ft/degrees	Structure Weight (lb)
'50s Indy roadster	Multi-tube	Steel	500-1,000	150
1954 F1 Maserati	Multi-tube	Steel	250	NA
'62 F1 Lotus	Space frame	Steel	1,000	72
'62 F1 Lotus	Monocoque	Aluminum	2,400	70
'66 F1 McLaren	Monocoque	Aluminum/balsa	11,000	NA
'68 STP Indy turbocar	Monocoque	Aluminum	>30,000	137
'79 F1 Lotus (early)	Monocoque	Aluminum	3,000	95
'80 F1 Lotus	Monocoque	Aluminum sandwich	10,000	75
'90 Indy March	Monocoque	Carbon fiber	>25,000	<90

Either the frame or the damper is in the wrong place—the junction of three tubes about a handspan behind and below where the damper attaches would be a natural mounting point. Also, the tube of this overhung mounting will itself bend considerably when the damper forces get big, which they will. *Harry Dunn*

Keeping the points where loads enter the frame as close as possible to the main structure is a much better idea. And ensuring that the brackets don't flex is nearly as im-portant as making the main structure stiff. *Robin Hartford, Open Wheel Magazine*

Chapter 12

The de Dion Axle

We have talked at length about slip angles, camber, roll centers, springs, anti-dive, and various other topics, but everything we have had to say boils down to a few simple bits of logic:

• A race car's handling—how fast it can get around a turn, and how controllable it is—depends on the forces its tires produce.

• Apart from the tires themselves, just two major factors affect those forces: the attitude of the tires relative to the ground, and how much force is holding them on the track.

• Those factors, in turn, depend on the suspension system.

Though independent
rear suspension is totally
foreign to most oval racers,
de Dion suspension represents
a kind of halfway step between
conventional live-axles and the
intimidating complexity of
an independent setup.

To put this understanding to practical use, however, you have to be able to *alter* these variables, and that's one of the problems with the beam axle setups found on most open-wheel racers. As with electronic engine controls, virtually nothing can be adjusted, so though it is hard to go far wrong with a beam axle, it is equally hard to gain a significant advantage. On the other hand, independent suspension offers opportunities to tailor a car's handling in ways unmatched by those of a solid axle, but it also provides many more ways to mess up.

One way to mess up is to graft an independent suspension onto the front of a chassis that has been optimized for solid axles at both ends. Usually, independent systems have lower roll centers than do beam axles, so in the process of changing from one type of suspension to another, the front roll center may end up lower than it was. If nothing else is changed, this will make the car loose. It may seem that the new front end sticks too well, but in fact, the lower roll center at the front forces the back end to work too hard.

Though independent suspension has made some inroads into oval track racing, the results often fail to justify the trouble, and its acceptance has been limited. One reason for this may simply be unfamiliarity—the lessons learned from years of experience with beam axles don't always apply to independent setups. Also, whereas beam axles can work pretty well with a willowy frame, a successful independent setup needs a stiff chassis—the stiffer the better. Another reason may be a tendency to copy, say, an Indy car suspension and apply it to a sprint car. Problems may arise with the translation. Finally, and perhaps most important, little advantage is to be gained from improving the bite at the front end if the back end is left unchanged, and it is the back end that has the toughest job and needs the most help.

That sounds like the beginning of a sales pitch for independent *rear* suspension, but if racers shy away from independent suspension for the front end partly because of its complexity, there seems little reason to hope they will embrace the even greater complication of independent suspension for the back end. If there was just some way to dial some camber and maybe even some toe-in into the rear tires, without having to abandon the idea of an axle beam and without having to design a completely new car...

Well, there is! It's not a new idea—in fact, it dates back to the turn of the century. And it's not even new to oval track racing—Harry Miller's sensational front-wheel-drive racers of the twenties used it. It's called de Dion (say "duh DEE on") suspension, and it offers some, uh, *solid* benefits.

To understand how a de Dion setup works, take a look at the first illustration in this chapter. The wheels are connected by a solid beam—called the de Dion axle or de Dion tube—curved or kinked to clear the center section. Note that this axle only locates the wheels—the power is delivered by half-shafts, with universal joints (U-joints), from a center section that is solidly mounted to the chassis. When the wheels move up and down, the axle

Fully independent rear suspension, as shown here, may seem intimidatingly complex to racers accustomed to solid axles, and it is difficult to adapt to an existing live-axle car. Independent suspension at either end may also demand changes to the other end of the car, essentially requiring an all-new chassis design. De Dion suspension offers a compromise. *Halibrand*

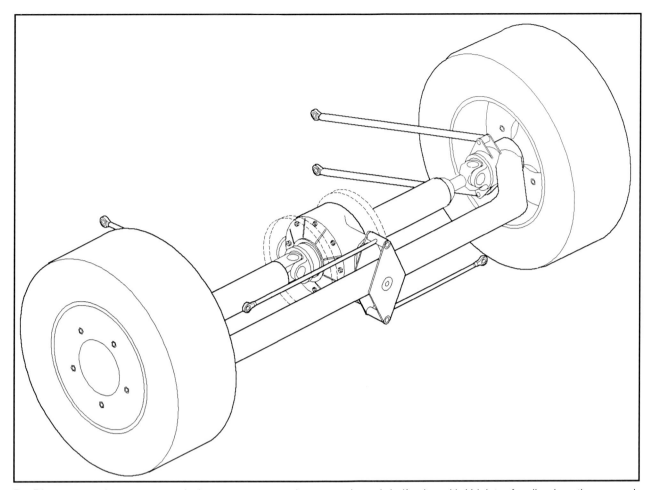

De Dion suspension uses an axle beam to connect the rear wheels together and to control their camber. The power is routed from a chassis-mounted center section through half axles with U-joints. A splined section on each half axle allows the axle to change length as the wheels move.

Another point favoring de Dion suspension is the reluctance of racers everywhere to stray too far from tried and true solutions.

moves with them but the center section stays put.

This suggests the first advantage of de Dion suspension: greatly reduced unsprung weight. Less machinery is flapping up and down with the wheels, which makes it easier for the springs and dampers to keep the tires planted. Also, since the center section doesn't bounce up and down with the wheels, the driver's seat may be mounted low-er, gaining the advantage, on pavement at least, of a lower center of gravity. A third advantage of de Dion suspension is the ability to adjust the camber and toe-in of the wheels. The U-joints that are nec-essary to allow the axle to move while the center section remains fixed also allow the wheels to be set at any camber or toe angle you desire.

Of course, some degree of camber is possible with a conventional solid axle—tire stagger does just that. Nine-and-a-half inches of stagger over a track width of 60in will produce nearly 1.5 degrees of camber. But stagger has some other important effects, and the amount that's best for helping the car snap into a turn is not likely to be the same as the amount that gives optimum camber for bite *in* the turn. Like an independent setup, de Dion sus-pension permits stagger to be changed without af-fecting a change in camber, and vice versa.

Another point favoring de Dion suspension is the reluctance of racers everywhere to stray too far from tried and true solutions. Race cars in Europe, for instance, were built about the same as in the

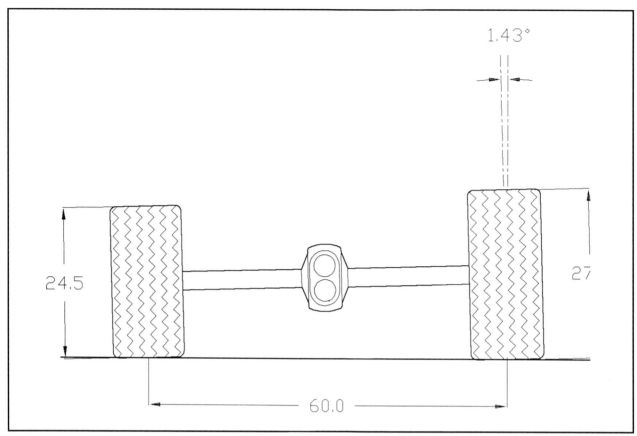

Stagger creates camber. Nine-and-a-half inches of difference in tire circumference yields nearly 1.5 degrees of camber. With a solid axle, camber and stagger cannot be adjusted separately. De Dion systems get around this.

United States, with solid axles at both ends, until the thirties. Independent front suspension came next, but the Europeans didn't just step directly from those to the current all-independent arrangements. From just before World War II until the late fifties—only ten racing years, when you subtract the war period—many of them ran with de Dion setups at the back. You could argue that this transitional step was necessary, not for technical reasons, but simply because there is a limit to how much change you can make in one step without exceeding people's psychological comfort level.

Though independent rear suspension is totally foreign to most oval racers, de Dion suspension represents a kind of halfway step between conventional live-axles and the intimidating complexity of an independent setup. Since the seventies, de Dion suspension has been used on Jim Hall's Chaparral 2H and on an exotic collection of street vehicles, including Aston Martins (such as the DBS), Rovers (such as the 2000), Maseratis, Alfa Romeos, and the Vector W8.

Perhaps the greatest advantage of de Dion suspension for oval track racers, then, is the relatively few changes needed to adapt it to a car with a conventional rear end. Springs, shocks, and most locat-

Though independent suspension has made some inroads into oval track racing, the results often fail to justify the trouble, and its acceptance has been limited. One reason for this may simply be unfamiliarity—the lessons learned from years of experience with beam axles don't always apply to independent setups.

ing links could be left where they are, helping to avoid the problem of a mismatch between front and rear suspensions that we suspect has a lot to do with the unpopularity of independent front ends.

A Watt's link for sideways location has been used in most de Dion installations, but a conventional Panhard rod or a "Jacob's ladder" could be used, or any other arrangement that might be applied to any beam axle. If a one-piece de Dion tube is used, one or both half axles obviously have to have a splined section to allow them to change length as the wheels move up and down. One neat alternative is to use the halfshafts themselves—U-jointed, but of fixed length—for lateral location, a tactic used by the English car maker Rover. To avoid "fighting" suspension movement, Rover put a slip joint in the middle of the de Dion tube. Using

fixed-length halfshafts also eliminates the problem of sliding splines binding up when handling lots of torque, which can—at its worst—effectively lock the suspension solid, trash the hub bearings, or punch in the side covers of the center section.

Another point: the de Dion axle doesn't need to be a large-diameter tube. As illustrated on these pages, a space frame structure can be used. That not only could save a bit of weight, but also could permit the "axle frame" to fit around all the other rear end machinery, while still giving clearance for bump and rebound movements. Maserati did something like this with one of its Le Mans cars.

The de Dion system is not perfect, of course. Like a live-axle, any kind of locating linkage that makes one wheel move forward (or backward) when it moves up (or down) will force the axle to

After being used in the nineteenth century for the rear suspension of several of Count de Dion's race and road cars, de Dion–type suspension was forgotten. It did not reappear until Harry Miller applied it to the front of his 91-cubic-inch Indy cars, starting in 1925. This 1928 Miller FWD, as driven by Leon Duray, clearly demonstrates the principle of locating a pair of wheels with a "dead" axle beam, while driving them with U-jointed half axles. *Jack Gladback*

skew in the frame, putting a steer angle into both rear wheels. It is possible to avoid this rear roll steer by using a linkage that provides straight-line motion, such as a Watt's link, to control the fore-aft location of the hubs. The only problem with this is that it prohibits building in any anti-squat effect. For anti-squat to work, the rear wheels have to move somewhat toward the rear as they roll up over bumps. Of course, rear roll steer can be used deliberately to modify the transient behavior of the car entering or exiting turns, so it may not be desirable to eliminate it.

In truth, it is *possible* to avoid rear steering when anti-squat is built into a de Dion setup, by making the hubs free to swivel—like steering knuckles—and then controlling the toe angle of the wheels through a separate linkage that keeps that angle constant when the axle moves back and forth. Even in its basic form, though, a de Dion system is a bit more complicated to make than a conventional setup, and this last recipe is probably just too complex to bother with.

Other drawbacks? A de Dion system may be a bit heavier in total than a conventional axle, though the difference shouldn't be much if the whole thing is properly engineered. As well, it is hard to use the torque reaction of the rear end to help increase the loading on the rear tires during acceleration. If the center section is mounted solidly to the chassis frame, the torque reaction just loads up the frame, without affecting tire loads. This is also true of fully independent rear suspensions, however, and some independent setups—the current Corvette, for instance—get around this to some extent.

On the 'Vette, the center section is allowed to pivot around a pair of mounts near the front of the pinion housing. Its transverse leaf ("buggy") spring, however, is mounted near the back of the center section, so when the power is turned on and the pinion tries to climb the ring gear, the housing twists downwards somewhat, taking the spring

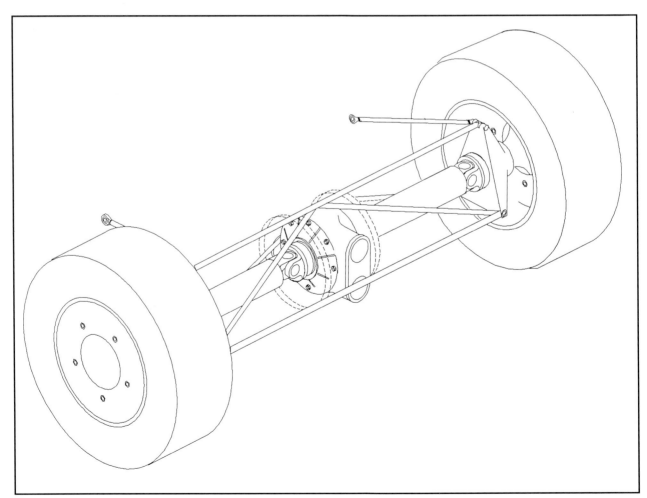

It is not necessary to use a single fat tube for a de Dion axle. A space frame axle will do the job with less weight, and possibly better packaging.

with it. That tends to jack up the back of the car and so adds some load to the rear tires. The same could be done with a de Dion axle.

Based on the experience of the road racers who used de Dion suspension, all this complication—finding some way around the axle steer effects and trying to use the rear end torque reaction to increase tire contact forces—is unnecessary. Earlier cars with every bit as much power and torque as that of a contemporary sprinter—though admittedly with quite a bit less tire—got along just fine with the simple arrangement shown in the first illustration, and worked way better with de Dion suspension than with the live-axles they replaced.

Though some of its applications have been very complex, reduced to its basics, the de Dion suspension is an entirely practical proposition, offering improved traction, especially on rough tracks, and the opportunity to separate the effects of stagger and camber. Best of all, it may be sufficiently straightforward and user friendly to encourage some racers to give it a try.

Apart from its use at the front of Harry Miller's front-wheel-drive screamers, de Dion suspension has appeared several times at the rear of Indy cars. The de Dion tube is just visible snaking under the overhung transmission of the Rounds Rocket Special that appeared at Indy in 1949. *Indy 500 photo*

Appendices

Suppliers

ADDCO Industries
672 Watertower Road
Lake Park, FL 33408

American Fabricating Co.
P.O. Box 548
Boonville, IN 47601

Aurora Bearing Co.
970 S. Lake St.
Aurora, IL 60506-5929

Carrera Shocks
5412 New Peachtree Rd.
Atlanta, GA 30341

Coleman Machine Inc.
N-1597 US 41
Menominee, MI 49858

Competition Engineering
P.O. Box 1470
Guilford, CT 06437

Dillon Enterprises, Inc.
6680 State Rd. 23
North Liberty, IN 46554

Ebeling Engineering
1438 Potrero Ave. So.
El Monte, CA 91733

Gambler Competition Center, Inc.
128 Volunteer Drive
Hendersonville, TN 37075

Halibrand
9344 Wheatlands Rd.
Santee, CA 92072

Keizer Aluminum Wheels
P.O. Box 50188
Phoenix, AZ 85076

Koni America
8085 Production Ave.
Florence, KY 41042

National Rod Ends
1920 Shawnee Rd.
Eagan, MN 55122

Precision Aerospace Research
929 E. Juanita Ave., Unit 104
Mesa, AZ 85284

8 Pro Shocks
1865 "A" Beaver Ridge Circle
Norcross, GA 30071

Sander Engineering
3155 Kashina Street
Torrance, CA 90505

Smoker Peformance
204 Bell Place
Woodstock, GA 30188

Speedway Motors
P.O. Box 81906
Lincoln, NE 68501-1906

Stallard Chassis Co.
123 Sandy Drive
Newark, DE 19713

Sweet Manufacturing, Inc.
3421 S. Burdick
Kalamazoo, MI 49001

Vette Products
7490 30th Ave.
St. Petersburg, FL 33710

Willwood Disc Brakes
461 Calle San Pablo
Camarillo, CA 93012

Selected Bibliography and Suggested Further Reading

Abbott, Ira H. & Albert E. von Doenhoff. *Theory of Wing Sections*. New York, 1959. Dover

Bastow, Donald. *Car Suspension and Handling*. London, 1980. Pentech

Bidwell, Joseph B. Vehicle directional control behavior described in more precise terms. *J SAE* February 1964

Bidwell, Joseph B. State of the art - vehicle control and road holding. *SAE 700366*

Campbell, Colin. *New Directions in Suspension Design*. Cambridge, MA, 1981. Robert Bentley

Costin, Michael & David Phipps. *Racing and Sports Car Chassis Design*. Cambridge, MA, 1962. Robert Bentley

Dominy, J.A. & R.G. Dominy. Aerodynamic influences on the performance of the Grand Prix racing car. *Proc. Instn Mech Engrs* v.198 no.7

Ellis, J.R. An introduction to the dynamic properties of vehicle suspensions. *Proc. Instn Mech Engrs* v.179 part 2A, no.3

Ellis, J.R. Understeer and oversteer. *Automobile Engineer* May 1963

Hoerner, Sighard F. *Fluid Dynamic Drag*. Vancouver, WA, 1965. Hoerner Fluid Dynamics

Hoerner, Sighard F. & H.V. Borst. *Fluid Dynamic Lift*. Albuquerque, NM, 1985. Mrs Liselotte Hoerner

Huntington, Roger. *Design and Development of the Indy Car*. Tucson, AZ, 1981. HP Books

Katz, Joseph. Investigation of negative lifting surfaces attached to an open wheel racing car configuration. *SAE 850283*

Katz, Joseph. Aerodynamic model for wing-generated down force on open wheel racing car configurations. *SAE 860218*

Liebeck, Robert H. Design of subsonic airfoils for high lift. *J. Aircraft* v.15 no.9

Liebeck, Robert H. On the design of subsonic airfoils for high lift. AIAA 9th Fluid & Plasma Dynamics Conf'ce

Lissaman, P.B.S. Low Reynolds number airfoils. *Ann. Rev. Fluid Mech* (1983)

McNay, G. & L. Southwick. An approximate lap time minimization based on Indy style racing car geometry. *SAE 910011*

Metz, L. Daniel. Aerodynamic properties of Indy cars. *SAE 870726*

Metz, L. Daniel. Aerodynamic requirements at the Indianapolis Motor Speedway. *J. Guidance* v.8 no.4

Miley, S.J. *A catalog of low Reynolds number airfoil data for wind turbine applications*. USDE Wind Energy Technology Dept

Nordeen, Donald L. Analysis of tire lateral forces and interpretation of experimental tire data. *SAE 670173*

Nye, Doug. *History of the Grand Prix Car 1966-1985*. Richmond, Surrey, 1986. Hazleton Publishing

Setright, L.J.K. *The Grand Prix Car 1954-1966*. New York, 1968. W.W. Norton & Co.

Smith, Carroll. *Tune to Win*. Fallbrook, CA, 1978. Aero Publishers

Steeds, W. *Mechanics of Road Vehicles*. London, 1960. Iliffe

Terry, Len & Alan Barker. *Racing Car Design and Development*. Croydon, Surrey, 1973. Motor Racing Publications

Van Valkenburgh, Paul. *Race Car Engineering and Mechanics*. New York, 1976. Dodd, Mead & Co.

Wright, P.G. The influence of aerodynamics on the design of Formula One racing cars. *Int J of vehicle design* v.3 no.4

Index